The Expansion of Social Work in Britain

LIBRARY OF SOCIAL WORK

GENERAL EDITOR: NOEL TIMMS
Professor of Applied Social Studies
University of Bradford

The Expansion of Social Work in Britain

Philip Seed

Senior Lecturer in Social Work
Department of Sociology, University of Aberdeen

LONDON AND BOSTON
ROUTLEDGE & KEGAN PAUL

734642

First published 1973
by Routledge & Kegan Paul Ltd
Broadway House, 68-74 Carter Lane,
London EC4V 5EL and
9 Park Street,
Boston, Mass. 02108, U.S.A.
Printed in Great Britain by
Northumberland Press Ltd
Gateshead
© Philip Seed 1973
ISBN 0 7100 7536 7 (c)
          7537 5 (p)
Library of Congress Catalog Card Number 72-90120

General editor's introduction

The Library of Social Work is designed to meet the needs of students following courses of training for social work. In recent years the number and kinds of training have increased in an unprecedented way. The Library will consist of short texts designed to introduce the student to the main features of each topic of enquiry, to the significant theoretical contributions so far made to its understanding, and to some of the outstanding problems. Each volume will suggest ways in which the student might continue his work by further reading.

The main argument of this essay is one of connection: social work can only be understood if the historical threads, usually separated for close scrutiny, are woven together again. This argument is pursued throughout this wide-ranging book. In the first part, Philip Seed describes the way in which social work as a movement (and such a characterisation is novel and useful) succeeded to the inheritance of philanthropy. It is the author's contention that this succession was aided by three forms of disciplined social action which characterised the nine-teenth century—social action within a developing system of social administration, the charity organisation move-ment, and direct social action. The second and third parts of the book are concerned with the more difficult task of interpreting more recent events in the social services. The author traces some of the influences on the expansion of social work after the Second World War, focusing especially on the development of Family Service Units and the conceptualisation of the problem family, which, as his analysis suggests, already has an old-fashioned air about it. Finally, three important themes are explored—the return of the volunteer, the relaxation of the political commitment to welfare, and the 'fashionable' topic of community work, though the author reminds us that it is difficult to think of any technique of modern community work which was not experimented with between 1895 and 1910.

We lack a good history of social work, even though it has been clear for some time that statements about the origins of social work, such as that it grew from Graeco-Romano, Christian roots, merely draw attention to the ignorance they are supposed to reduce. Two kinds of historical enquiry are required: the close, patient study of certain crucial relationships (for example, the influence exerted by Chalmers on the Charity Organisation Society), and the interpretation of broad developments in social work. Philip Seed's essay belongs to the second category. It helps us to begin restoration work on the historical face of social work not because it is a detailed, comprehensive history, but because it offers interpretations of the origins of social work and its expansion up to the present which should succeed at least in encouraging some arguments about the historical development and contemporary status of social work.

NOEL TIMMS

Contents

CONTENTS

viii

Introduction

This book is not a comprehensive history of social work. The historical material used is selected to focus on aspects of certain periods of social history in order to develop an understanding (and as objective an understanding as possible) of what modern social work 'is', and of what the rapid expansion of social work today 'means' as a social phenomenon.

One of the difficulties in writing about the history of social work is that social work is a relatively modern term. Sociology, social science and social reform are older terms. Some social workers and some historians ignore this problem and write confidently about social work in the nineteenth century, the seventeenth century, or even social work in biblical times. According to one recent writer Bessel (1970): 'The earliest social work model that we know, which is similar to our own, is described in the Acts of the Apostles.' Bessel also writes: 'The first century manuals for the instruction of the deacons, who were primarily *social workers*, have a very modern flavour' (*my italics*). What does this mean? The prize for pseudo-history, however, should perhaps go to Goetschius (Kuenstler, 1961):

> Community organisation ... is no new discovery or recent innovation ... the social welfare needs of the individual and the family in community were studied in the Code of Hammurabi, in the Confucian, the Vedic, the Buddhist and the Egyptian Scriptures, in the Old Testament, by Plato and Aristotle, by the Roman Jurists, the Church Fathers, and the Mediaeval schoolmen.

Young and Ashton (1956) say in their Preface: 'By social work we do not mean social reform ... We use the term social work as referring to the personal efforts of individuals who assist those in distress or promote the welfare of those unsuccessful in promoting their own.' To make these sorts of assumptions surely amounts to reading history backwards? There is a difference between trying to understand the historical background to events and traditions from which there is evidence that ideas about modern social work developed—which is what we shall be trying to do—and simply claiming a piece of history as belonging to modern social work.

We shall also try to avoid the temptation to take up in advance a particular interpretation of modern social work, and therefore of its historical antecedents, in order to justify a favourite sociological perspective. Halmos (1965), for example, in order to place social workers in a category he calls 'counsellors' (who have taken on the mantle of caring for people in a society tired of religious and political solutions to social problems) assumes, by implication, that the therapeutic role of the social worker is paramount and historically the most significant. We should make no such assumptions. Other interpretations of modern social work and of what is, and what is not, historically significant can be made. For example, an American writer, Lubove (1966) considers that the 'distinctive' function of social work in an 'atomised urban society' is not 'therapy' but 'liaison between groups and the stimulation of legislation'. An Indian writer, Gore

(1957), includes 'the leader of ideas' in a list of the usages of the term 'social work'.

All that one can say at the outset is that in recent years various different groups of people have found the term 'social work' useful to describe the activities or the work they engaged in or shared in common with others. These have included non-professional as well as professional social workers. One cannot—and we do not—forget the former group.

The book is divided into three parts. In Part I we examine the traditions and the forms of social action in the nineteenth century from which social work originated. In Part II we move to the period following the Second World War and concentrate particularly on the development of family casework in relation to what was sometimes called 'the problem of the problem family'. In Part III we examine the context of the recent expansion of social work in Britain into the field of community work.

Acknowledgments

I wish to acknowledge the assistance of the following in connection with the preparation of this book: David Jones, O.B.E., Walter Birmingham, Toynbee Hall, Family Service Units, Michael Lyon and Professor Noel Timms.

P.S.

PART I

Social conflict and the origins of social work

1
The philanthropic tradition and the national image

The term 'social work' was first used in Britain at the end of the nineteenth century in connection with the activities of people who had a sense of belonging to a movement which aimed at social advance based on disciplined and principled forms of social action. Social work was an attempt to find more realistic remedies to social problems and to social distress than traditional forms of philanthropy and charity.

Philanthropy and charity

These were both much older terms than social work. Philanthropy was the activity of giving away money for the public good. The philanthropist was a wealthy man who was 'public spirited'. Charity was the object for which the money was given.

The scale of philanthropy was impressive. From Tudor times until the end of the nineteenth century it was a social necessity for large sections of the upper and middle classes. The charitable objects of philanthropy covered a wide range of what we would nowadays call social services including, for example, schools, hospitals, apprenticeships and aid to prisoners, as well as specifically religious causes.

The machinery for dispensing charity varied. It included established institutions within the churches, associations and private trusts specially created for charitable purposes, and private individuals acting on their own initiative. Parliament allowed these activities to flourish, in some ways promoted them, but did not attempt to regularise them or co-ordinate their efforts into anything like a national social policy. Charity existed alongside the official system of poor relief and, in dealing with poverty, it was often considered more significant. Speaking of the period from 1480 to 1660 Jordan (1960), an authority on the subject, says: 'Though remedial legislation was adopted it was our conclusion that men of the age reposed their principal confidence in private charity, gathered through the instrumentality of the private trust into large and disciplined aggregates of wealth with which formidably effective social institutions could be founded and endowed.'

The social theories and the objectives of charity varied with the age. The emphasis was sometimes on the act of giving: to secure felicity to the giver or as a responsibility of stewardship that went with the right to accumulate wealth. At other times a greater emphasis was placed on the charitable objective such as a recognised need amongst the poor, the misfits or other groups, or in a national emergency for the population more generally. Charity could be seen as part of a permanent duty to relieve the poor who must always exist in society just as there should always be rich people or it was part of a utopian scheme to end poverty altogether. It could be either parochial or 'universal' in its appeal. The most significant facts about philanthropy are its permanence, importance and ubiquitous existence in town and country alike over a long period of more than 300 years.

Boulding's concept of the 'image' applied to philanthropy

To understand further the role of philanthropy and charity as social institutions in Britain from which social work developed, we will use Boulding's concept of 'the image' (1958): 'What I am talking about ... is what I believe to be true; my subjective knowledge. It is this image that largely governs my behaviour.' In applying the concept to the political process he suggests the importance of 'symbolic images' and 'value images' which serve as a kind of 'rough summation or index of a vast complexity of images of roles and structures'. Similar ideas are discussed in relation to international affairs by Seed (1966), and, in relation to the welfare state by Titmuss (in Schottland, 1967).

Boulding is particularly concerned with symbolic images of 'other nations' posing a threat to the security of one's own nation as part of the process by which ideal national images of society based on 'freedom', 'justice', or whatever, are sustained. We can use this kind of analysis to understand the role of philanthropy. For at least three centuries philanthropy suggested symbolic images which both sustained current value images (varying from decade to decade) and hid uncomfortable realities which, if exposed, would threaten established national institutions in general. For example, philanthropy as the display of wealth could help to sustain images of a prosperous and free nation; and prosperity and freedom to which the total population could subscribe, could serve to hide uncomfortable realities about the unequal distribution of wealth and power within the nation.

It is interesting to note the titles of well-known charitable enterprises because they conveyed some of these images. 'The Society for the Reformation of Manners' must have helped to sustain an eighteenth-century ideal image of a well-mannered, reasonable and, above all, a well-ordered English society. (It could, perhaps, be argued that the Society for the Reformation of Manners was not typical of charitable organisations. 'The Societies purposed to raise the tone of public morals by directing against offenders [turned in by Society informers armed with sheaves of warrants] the force of the criminal law' (Owen, 1965). The significant point, however, as Owen points out, is that 'the foremost philanthropists of the age were warm supporters of the Crusade.')

The political significance of philanthropy and charity was that they over-simplified social problems and social conflict, and served as a brake against too rapid political change. How comforting if everybody could believe that the complex problems of the agrarian revolution and of the early stages of the industrial revolution could be simplified down to the reformation of morals, as represented by 'manners'! The charity and philanthropic scene was like a stage for acting out comforting and comfortable answers to complex social problems in villages, country estates, small towns and growing cities as well as nationally.

This is not to deny the importance of individual actors whose ideas for reform were sometimes well ahead of the accepted ideas of their contemporaries—such as, for example, John Bellers whose ideas in the late seventeenth century anticipated many features of twentieth-century social provision; Mary Wolstoncroft in the eighteenth who stood for equal rights for women; or Robert Owen in the nineteenth century. But their parts did not alter the social significance of the play as a whole. Philanthropy served to display wealth, and charity over-simplified social need and social conflict. The play expressed social problems in individual, interpersonal, and often, symbolic terms. Sometimes the actors exposed fresh social needs but these, too, became simplified in the sense that they were seen in terms of a personal charitable transaction between the philanthropist, or his agent, and the recipient.

We can now apply this idea more specifically to charity

in the nineteenth-century situation which gave rise to the development of social work as a movement.

The nineteenth century

Philanthropy in the nineteenth century was on a scale greater than ever before. So, too, were the total population, the size of cities, the rapidity of social change, the scale of economic exploitation and the gap between the richest and the poorest citizens. To give just one example, David Owen gives an account of the activities of Baroness Burdett-Coutts (1814-1906) who, at the age of twenty-three inherited an unearned *income* (not capital) of £80,000 a year. The total weekly earnings of a working-class family at that time were in the region of £1 to £1·50. She gave large amounts of money away, including £50,000 at one time. The charitable objects in which she was particularly interested ranged from child welfare and education to housing betterment schemes, fallen women, colonial bishoprics and the Irish potato famine (Owen, 1965).

The ideal national narcissistic images of the nineteenth century were of progress, expansion and wealth. The political system survived in spite of intermittent fears of a revolution. After the Napoleonic wars there was no longer an external threat. The Empire grew. Britain was the workshop of the world. All this was expressed in the Great Exhibition of 1851. The ideal images were sustained partly by philanthropic activity but also by a social philosophy based on the idea of a 'free market economy' (which, of course, never completely existed) in which Man's 'self-love' was God's 'providence'. Wages and prices were supposed to adjust naturally to the mutual benefit of employer and labourer, of producer and consumer. Automatic mechanisms were supposed to control the creation of money and free trade was supposed to ensure ever greater and ever wider prosperity (Polanyi, 1957).

In relation to this philosophy, philanthropy was seen as both a blessing and a curse. It was a blessing in that it showed what wealth there was to spare and, in general, it expressed images of hope. On the other hand, philanthropy was a curse in that it interfered with the ideal operation of the free labour market. By scrounging from many charities and living off the philanthropy of the rich, the labourer could escape the natural operation of the free market. Philanthropy, unless strictly controlled, was often seen, indeed, as the cause of the social ill it sought to remedy.

This was not entirely a new idea. Indiscriminate giving had often been seen as inconsistent with the principle of self-help which, it was recognised, should be encouraged. However, what had previously been an ethical question of personal responsibility was turned, in the nineteenth century, into an economic argument. If people did not learn to help themselves it was supposed that the economic order to society would be upset and this, in turn, among other things, would lead to an increase in poverty. Thus it was thought that philanthropy could actually increase poverty. It was seen to be both morally and economically degrading. The exceptional poor, who might be 'deserving', could legitimately be helped when the possibilities of self-help within the family or local community had been exhausted, but the 'undeserving' poor, the pauper, should be economically deterred.

Charity in the nineteenth century developed either within the context of these ideas or as a challenge to them from those, like Robert Owen, who believed that society was at fault and that the social system and its philosophy were wrong.

By the end of the nineteenth century, philanthropy was losing its credibility as a major social institution for remedying social distress. The effectiveness and the relevance of the traditional charitable transaction were being questioned. So, too, were the national images of progress and prosperity which philanthropy had helped to sustain. Despite the unparalleled accumulation of wealth, seemingly miraculous scientific advances, the accomplishment of successful geographical exploration, and improved means of communication, social advance had not kept pace. The benefits of progress were unevenly shared. These sentiments were expressed in the Majority Report of the Poor Law Commission in 1909 (quoted in Rose, 1971):

'Land of Hope and Glory' is a popular and patriotic lyric sung each year by thousands of voices. The enthusiasm is partly evoked by the beauty of the idea itself, but more by the belief that Great Britain does, above all other countries, merit this eulogium ... To certain classes of the community into whose moral and material condition it has been our duty to explore, these words are a mockery and a falsehood ... No country, however rich, can permanently hold its own in the race of international competition, if hampered by an increasing load of this dead weight; or can successfully perform the role of sovereignty beyond the seas, if a portion of its own folk at home are sinking below the civilisation and aspirations of its subject races abroad ...

Great Britain is the home of voluntary effort, and its triumphs and successes constitute in themselves much of the history of the country. But voluntary effort when attacking a common and ubiquitous evil must be disciplined and led. We have here to learn a lesson ...

Social work came into being closely related to a need to repair the national image of greatness which had been spoilt through the dramatic exposure of social need at the end of the nineteenth century, and where charity and philanthropy had failed. We will be examining this in more detail in chapter 3. Before we do this, however, in chapter 2 we will consider the particular forms of social action in the nineteenth century upon which social work practice was built.

2

Disciplined social action
in the nineteeth century

Frederick Engels's famous book, *The Condition of the Working Classes in England*, provides an analysis as well as a vivid description of some of the worst, but nevertheless widespread, social conditions in Britain in 1844. Today available as a paperback (Hobsbawm, 1969), it was originally available only in German, and was not published in Britain until 1892. In the 1890s there developed an interest in understanding the causes of social problems and in facing up to the extent of social degradation in a supposedly prosperous society. At this time of mounting interest in social enquiry, the term social work came into being and signified participation in a social movement pledged to what was called social advance.

Barry McLaughlin, Herbert Blumer, Wendell King and others, in *Studies in Social Movements* (McLaughlin, 1969), provide some useful conceptual frameworks for considering social movements. Blumer defines social movements as 'collective enterprises to establish a new order of life', and King as 'a group venture extending beyond a local community or a single event and involving a systematic effort to inaugurate changes in thought, behaviour and social relationships'. Blumer distinguishes between general social movements and specific movements, and between revolutionary movements and reform movements. His statement about a reform movement particularly applies to social work. A reform movement derives support from the prevailing code of ethics and 're-affirms the ideal values of a society'. When the term 'social work' was first used, it related to a conscious effort to re-affirm the ideal values of late Victorian and Edwardian society. Yet, fifty years previously, when the *Condition of the Working Classes* was first written, and when their condition was very much worse than in 1892, many people who were better off used traditional philanthropy as a way of avoiding the reality. Social statistics existed in the first half of the nineteenth century to an extent which could have made possible a greater awareness of social distress at that time. The first census was held in 1801. The first English statistical societies were formed in the 1830s (Kirkman-Gray, 1908). Rather than examine social statistics it was easier to glory in the tradition of philanthropy itself. As David Owen (1965) says, speaking of the mid-century:

> For most Englishmen the hundreds of charitable institutions represented one of the glories of the British tradition and stood as a monument to the superiority of voluntary action over State intervention. They were warmed by an instinctive glow of pride as they contemplated the magnitude of British resources dedicated to the improvement of British life.

The part played by philanthropists in Victorian society was, however, complex (Harrison, 1966). Sometimes philanthropists were associated with political reform movements, such as the long struggle for the control of factory hours, the movement for a state system of elementary education, or the extension of the franchise. Others were more concerned with social action than with political action and it is from among these people, the work they did and the principles they held, that influences leading to the particular characteristics of social work can be traced. In this chapter we will consider these influences, based on particular and very different forms of disciplined social action, under three headings: first, *social action within a developing system of social administration*; second, *the charity organisation movement*; and third, forms of social action, less easy to define because of the diversity of context, but nevertheless identifiable in terms of principles of action, which we will call *direct social action*.

Social action within a developing system of social administration

According to one interpretation of the tenets of a *laissez faire* philosophy, it was an anomaly to have any system of positive social administration at all. For this reason, *The Times*, for example, was opposed to the beginnings of a more centralised Poor Law in 1834 (Rose, 1971):

> This Poor Law system is an invention only ... No seed or sprig of it is to be found in the records of our ancient history ... In one word, it is AGAINST the deep-rooted and long-formed habits of this nation, the principle of all which is that the people should be made to govern themselves as much as possible, at least in their domestic concerns and relations.

On similar grounds, a little later, *The Times* opposed state intervention in the field of public health. Nevertheless professional administration entered these fields. In the Poor Law Administration it attempted to systematise and control relief, which, before 1834, had got out of hand when lay parish guardians had tried to curb social unrest by subsidising very low wages and paying out what amounted to a kind of family allowance. This was the so-called Speenhamland system. Although at first popular, it was later considered disastrous both to the employer and to the labourer.

The employer was encouraged to pay artificially low

wages knowing that they would be supplemented out of relief funds. The benefits to the labourer were short-lived since relief rates could be, and were, arbitrarily reduced. The relief paid out came from local rates. It was perhaps of more importance than is generally recognised, however, in forcing the Poor Law Commission of 1832 to consider, if only to reject, the proposition that the state should be, as the Commission put it, 'the general insurer against misfortune, idleness, improvidence and vice' (Lubove, 1966).

Professional social administration entered public health when outbreaks of cholera brought home to some of the rich the need for effective sanitation amongst the poor, and in relation to mental illness because insanity afflicted the higher as well as the lower orders of society. In all these cases, an underlying dilemma was how to reconcile a reluctance to interfere in what was officially recognised as the natural order of society with a desire to be scientific and efficient in necessary measures of control and in accordance with an image of progress. The only acceptable basis for bureaucratic intervention was a reluctant need for control; but investigations arising from this need led on by stages to forms of positive social provision. In this process the professional social administrator came into being and performed an increasingly important role in relation to social action.

The Poor Law Amendment Act of 1834 was a compromise between the desire for system and the desire for no system. Its underlying philosophy, of deterring people from pauperism by threatening them with having to leave their homes and enter a workhouse as a condition of being fed, was unevenly and inconsistently applied. Having, in some cases, broken up families and separated parents from children, the administration became concerned that pauper children should be educated. Poor Law Boards, by and by, started schools which, in some cases, as at Manchester, managed to attract staff concerned to

13

experiment with enlightened educational methods (Rose, 1971).

The social administrator achieved a skill in promoting social reform while subscribing to social control. The most famous of those to whom this applied was Edwin Chadwick. As one of the chief architects of the Poor Law of 1834, he preached the necessity for the social control of pauperism. Yet he began a crusade for reform in the field of public health which led him to expose slum conditions which, he insisted, had to be changed before it would be reasonable to expect the Poor Law principles to operate effectively. In so doing he implicitly recognised that social problems could not be accounted for purely in terms of defects in personal character, although the Poor Law was supposed to operate on the principle that they could! Chadwick wrote (Gregg, 1970):

> I deem it to be an important principle to be borne in mind that in the actual condition of the lower classes, conveniences [of water supplies] ... must precede and form habits [of the working classes] ... It is in vain to expect [of] the great majority of them that the disposition, still less the habits, will precede or anticipate and create the conveniences.

To drive the point home further, he says that even when the middle classes have an interruption to their water supplies through frozen pipes, they, too, become demoralised, 'and when it is necessary to send for water to a distance, the house cleansings and washings are diminished by the inconvenience' (Gregg, 1970).

The successful efforts of Chadwick and of others in the public health movement demonstrated the possibility of reform generated from within the system of administration itself and supported from outside. The social administrators believed in the possibility of reform through parliament and they played an important role in producing many reports and other documents based on official statistics which were in the long run effective in educating public opinion in favour of the need for social legislation and for its effective implementation.

Social administrators also played a role in promoting social experiments within the system of statutory services, and some of these were quite as remarkable as many of the better known voluntary experiments. In the field of mental health, for example, Hanwell hospital under official auspices was as much ahead of its time in treatment methods as the more famous voluntary hospital, The Retreat, started earlier by the Quakers. The Retreat is normally regarded as having been progressive (Jones, 1955) but, for an opposite view, see Foucault (1967). In the field of juvenile justice, Parkhurst was operating on enlightened lines at the same time as Mary Carpenter's first voluntary experiments (Carlebach, 1970). A key role in linking statutory and voluntary effort was that of the inspectors. Some of the people attracted to these posts were committed to promoting positive social provision and experimentation. An example was Mrs Jane Elizabeth Senior, who was the first woman to be appointed to the Poor Law inspectorate. In 1873 she produced an influential report strengthening the case for the wider adoption in England of the Scottish system of boarding out children in preference to the policy of confining them in large institutions. We quote this as an example of an inspector's report advocating changes in social provision (Rose, 1971):

> In the course of this tour I visited several sets of children boarded out in different districts ... I received the same impression everywhere, in favour of the free and natural mode of life afforded by cottage homes. I did not see a single case of ringworm or ophthalmia and the children, almost without exception looked strong and thriving and happy ... It would, in my opinion, be an inestimable benefit to the orphans now being educated at the Metropolitan pauper schools, to be placed under the boarding out system; provided, of course, that it were properly carried out.

15

The social administrators of the nineteenth century were important in relation to the subsequent development of social work for three main reasons. First, they constituted a link, not always a very popular one, between voluntary charitable effort and political action. Second, their experience in innovation, while at the same time acting as agents of social control, provided a pattern for subsequent statutory social action. Third, their administrative experience in social investigation in preparing reports, working in teams, and in establishing viable forms of bureaucratic organisation, helped to make the idea of collective social service provision in Britain a credible one at the end of the nineteenth century.

The charity organisation movement

The charity organisation movement was an attempt, first, to define charity in terms of scientific method and, second, to organise philanthropy effectively so as to be able to tackle social problems by this method. It shared with the supporters of the 1834 Poor Law the fear of indiscriminate relief, and it sought to co-operate with the Poor Law system. On the other hand, it represented an alternative to the Poor Law in so far as charity, by definition, was an individual, personal act which no agency of the state could perform. As the President of the Poor Law Board, G. J. Goschen put it, in the same year (1869) that the Charity Organisation Society was formed: 'The fundamental doctrine of the English Poor Laws was that relief was given not as a matter of charity, but of legal obligation ... Therefore it should only be given in cases of actual destitution.' But the role of charitable organisations, 'whose aims could in no way be considered as a right', was to prevent the necessity for increasing the numbers dependent on the Poor Law. Charity organisations would find 'their most appropriate sphere in assisting those who have some, but insufficient, means' (Rose, 1971).

The charity organisation movement was wider than the Charity Organisation Society, but the COS, as it was called, under the leadership of its energetic secretary, C. S. Loch, was the means of propagating a set of principles which governed scientific charity. These principles were reiterated in various forms and the following is a summary (Woodroofe, 1966):

1. No work of charity is complete which does not place the person benefited in self-dependence.
2. All means of pressure must be brought to bear upon the individual to help or force him into being self-dependent, e.g. shame, influence of relatives.
3. The family is to be considered as a whole.
4. A thorough knowledge is necessary both of the circumstances of the persons seeking help and of the means of helping them.
5. Relief, to effect a cure, should be adequate in kind and quantity.

These principles were not new. Local visiting societies, such as the Brighton Charity Society started by Elizabeth Fry, had much earlier tried to bring discipline to charitable practice. Certain groups, for example the Quakers and the Jews, had a long tradition of promoting self-help within their own communities. Within the Quaker system of Monthly Meetings, for example (Jorns, 1931),

any person in need of help could apply to the Meeting personally or through some other Member. But in order that persons who needed help, but were too timid or proud to say so, should not suffer actual want, the elders and overseers or, sometimes, visiting committees specially appointed for the purpose, had the duty of watching continuously over the circumstances of all the members, and of reporting cases which in their judgement needed help to the next Monthly Meeting ... An attempt was first made to secure the co-operation of members of the family, for whom remunerative work

17

was secured in order to make it possible for them to contribute. Not until this plan proved impracticable did the Meeting step in.

Within the Church of Scotland, Dr Chalmers developed a visiting scheme somewhat similar, though harsher, in the 1820s, which, towards the end of the nineteenth century, was held up as a model within the COS. If an individual suffered misfortune so that he appeared unable to support himself, personal investigation was instituted to discover how the 'fountain' (to use Chalmer's phraseology) of charity could flow from the 'springs' of relatives or neighbourhood.

According to David Owen (1965), the Charity Organisation Society largely failed to achieve its stated objectives. Some bodies, for example the Salvation Army, had as little to do with it as possible. Its efforts to investigate individual cases were seldom effectively co-ordinated with Poor Law Boards. It was never operating on such a scale nor using such methods as could possibly bring it into contact with the full extent of social need nor with the full range of charitable effort it set out to organise. Nevertheless it had a widespread and long-lasting influence. It kept thorough records and it was effective in explaining its work and above all its 'principles'. The significance of these principles was that they re-inforced those aspects of charitable practice which were consistent with the image of scientific method and, with the force of an organised movement, this emphasis led to the beginnings of professional training. At first, training was to equip volunteers; later, it was to equip full-time workers to organise volunteers and, later still, to equip full-time professional social workers who replaced some of the volunteers. The COS provided an organisational setting conducive to professionalisation. The visitor was encouraged to be resourceful in what would, nowadays, be called a 'front-line' management situation, while compensatory controls from the centre took the form of supportive supervision based on completed records.

The influence of the charity organisation movement and, in particular, of the cos on the development of social work has been described frequently in social work literature (for example, Woodroofe, 1966). In our view, its importance has tended to be exaggerated. This is because emphasis has been placed on the development of social work as a profession based, first and foremost, on casework, at the expense of considering social work as a movement based more broadly on 'social advance'. (The cos was important in this respect too, as Mowat (1961) points out, although it did not succeed in giving this impression to its critics, such as the Webbs.) Insufficient attention, in our view, by comparison, has been given to other influences and forms of social action in the nineteenth century, and we will consider some of these now under the heading 'direct social action'.

Direct social action

Direct social action consisted in personal involvement beyond the point of established conventions. We shall consider this is relation to the activities and ideas of three well-known individuals in the nineteenth century: Robert Owen, Elizabeth Fry, Mary Carpenter, and one less well-known, William Watson. These four had, in some ways, different views of society and they were concerned with different social institutions. Yet they shared certain principles of social action. For example, they rejected the conventional idea that the individual pauper or the delinquent could be blamed for the problems of society. Society, too, was to blame. There was therefore no point in distinguishing, as the cos did in its early days, between the deserving and the undeserving—the undeserving needed attention too. A better approach was to attempt to recast the institutions of society in terms which gave direct expression to charity as 'the universal law of love'. They advocated radical changes but not violent revolution. They were usually opposed to punishment. They were only incidentally interested in legislative reforms and they were largely dissociated from political movements aimed at action through parliament. The basis of their alternative action was twofold : first, they believed in the possibility of global changes occurring from parochial beginnings based on individual example; and, second, they believed in the possibility of change through persuasion based on a rational view of fellow human beings.

In using the description 'direct social action', we need to distinguish two other related, though different, concepts. The first is 'direct action' either in the syndicalist sense or in the modern sense of non-violent resistance to political or racial tyranny (Carter, 1970). The second is 'voluntary action', as used by Beveridge (1948). In a book with this title, Beveridge analysed the contribution of individuals who voluntarily rendered public service in promoting social reform. This category is wider than 'direct social action'. Lord Shaftesbury, for example, is included in Beveridge's list, but he would not be included under the heading of direct social action in that he was primarily a parliamentarian. He served as a link between philanthropic effort (being an office-bearer and president of many associations) and the promotion of factory and other legislation, especially concerning the protection of children.

It is true that Robert Owen also, at one stage, tried to bring about reform in parliament, but this was incidental. His main purpose was to demonstrate, in a succession of experiments, the possibility of recreating the institutions of society on the principle of charity. His philosophy, as the following extracts from his autobiography suggest, was a philosophy of action, based on example (Kelley, 1967):

Hitherto the world has been tormented by useless talk-

ing ... Henceforward acting will render precepts un-
necessary and, in future, systems for the government
of mankind will be estimated and valued by their effects
in practice only.

I had now to commence the great experiment ...
This was, to ascertain whether the character of man
could be better formed, and society better constructed
and governed, by falsehood, fraud, force and fear, keeping him in ignorance and slavery to superstition—or by
truth, charity, and love based on an accurate knowledge
of human nature and by forming all the institutions of
society in accordance with that knowledge.

Owen's millennialism was coupled with a very practical
sense of the inter-relatedness of social needs. It was not
enough to institute a revolutionary system of personnel
management at New Lanark. He also instituted comprehensive health and welfare schemes and, to him, the most
important event, the opening in 1816 of an educational
institution which included his famous nursery school for
children aged two onwards.

The parents, at first, could not understand what I was
going to do with their little children at two years of
age, but seeing the results produced they became eager
to send their infants at one year old, and enquired if I
could not take them yet younger (Kelley, 1967).

The school was part of a total community plan in which
education was a community process.

It might seem a long way from Robert Owen the
socialist, trade unionist, co-operator, and radical to Elizabeth Fry, the saintly, humble Quaker, especially if one
remembers that Owen was also atheist and, at one stage,
anti-marriage! Yet in terms of their interpretation of the
principles of charity as a basis for social action they were
much closer. At different times, and especially at New
Lanark, Owen associated with a number of Quakers but
it is interesting that whereas, in his autobiography, he

criticises most Quakers for their sectarianism, he has nothing but praise for Elizabeth Fry, whose work he publicised apparently to the latter's embarrassment (Corder, 1853). Elizabeth Fry was accustomed to taking visitors on her rounds at Newgate and one of these was Robert Owen. The following account by Owen is interesting in telling us about the ideas both Owen and Fry shared (Kelley, 1967):

> I shall not easily, if ever, forget the impressions I experienced. In passing from room to room we were met in every instance (there was not one exception) with kind looks and the most evident feelings of affection in every prisoner towards Mrs. Fry. Not a feature in the countenance of any, however hardened they might have been on entering the prison, that did not evince a stronger expression than language can define, their love and admiration for what she had done for them ... She spoke in manner and voice the language of kindness, and commiseration, to each; and she was replied to in such accordant feelings as are, and ever will be, produced in human beings, whenever they shall be spoken to, and treated thus rationally.

Elizabeth Fry wrote of her own methods: 'The visitor must go in a spirit, not of judgement, but of mercy ... All female officers in prisons should be gentle yet firm ... The women under her can fully communicate a knowledge of their circumstances and pour forth their sorrows as to a wise and sympathetic friend.' Elizabeth Fry is best known for her work in prisons, and as a pioneer in nursing, but she applied her principles of social action based on personal relationships to other areas of charitable interest. She was especially concerned with people she thought might be lonely including, as well as those within institutions, shepherds and lighthouse keepers and, of course, convicts about to be transported to Australia (Witney, 1937). (Many of the convicts who received the attention of Fry and her helpers before embarkation were being punished for what amounted to political offences for reasons of conscience (of which the best known but by no means the only ones were the Tolpuddle Martyrs). There is, however, no evidence of any awareness on Fry's part of the political implications of relieving the suffering of prisoners who were, in some cases, as much the victims of persecution as many Quakers had once been.) In contrast to Owen, Fry never indulged in grandiose claims, but more simply described her aims as 'to do good and to communicate' (Witney, 1937). But mild in manner as she might be, she inherited the Quaker traditional confidence of 'speaking truth to power', and much of her success was attributed to the boldness and directness of her approach to authority, not least as a woman.

Mary Carpenter was less modest, but no less direct. Whereas Fry's ideas about social action developed in the context of a Quaker background, Carpenter, a generation later, was a Unitarian. The Unitarians had a visiting system similar to the Quakers for helping the poor and it was here that Mary Carpenter first developed a social concern to investigate more deeply into social problems. As with Owen and Fry, investigation led to social action based on personal example and commitment, of which Red Lodge Reformatory School is best known.

Modern writers tend to do those in the nineteenth century committed to direct social action the dis-service of fragmenting their areas of concern in accordance with twentieth-century concepts. Mary Carpenter's interests included not only reformatory and industrial schools but a whole range of neighbourhood services associated with the schools, such as an adult school, a lodging house for boys, and a home-visiting service, as well as wider interests such as unemployment, slavery in America, and the position of women in India. Her attitude to campaigning about women's rights in this country was typical of the ideas of direct social action. She is reported to have said (Carpenter, 1879): 'I don't talk about my rights—I take them.'

23

Mary Carpenter has been criticised for using statistics to suit her own views while claiming to be scientific (Carlebach, 1970). As with Owen, Carpenter claimed to base social action on scientific knowledge, although her understanding of 'science' was based on revealed truth rather than empirical data. The theme of revealed truth was charity, from which were derived 'laws' of human nature and of relationships. Thus Carpenter (1879) defined charity as 'undaunted faith in the divine purpose of each individual soul, the love that must blend with firmness and wisdom, the insight into the laws of child nature and the conflicts of a child's life'. As with Owen, the idea of 'revengeful punishments' was abhorrent to her. 'Children', she said, 'do not owe retribution to society, but society owes retribution to them.'

William Watson (1796-1887) is less known. His name is associated with industrial feeding schools which were started in Aberdeen and which later spread throughout Scotland and influenced the development of industrial schools in England. Up to a point, he was a conventional liberal of the Church of Scotland in which there was a tradition of social service. He helped to establish a Board of Health in Aberdeen in 1831, and played an active part in it during the cholera outbreak. A little later he helped to found a House of Refuge for vagrants in the City. Yet these activities did not seem to him to be enough, and he wrote in his diary: 'What have I done for my fellow men? Nothing! Nothing! Nothing!' His activities were subsequently less conventional (Angus, 1913).

As a Sheriff he was confronted with the problem of large numbers of juvenile pickpockets who roamed the streets. The only remedy within the penal system was imprisonment which was so harsh that children were sometimes deliberately not apprehended. Yet nothing constructive was done either. Watson's view was that 99 per cent of children who committed crimes did so as a necessary means of livelihood. The causes of juvenile

24

crime, he said, lay in poverty, and poverty was created by social conditions.

Watson's answer, which he personally put into practice, was to involve the community in a scheme to feed and educate delinquent children. His early schools were day schools, so that 'children carried home the lessons taught ... applying themselves diligently to cleaning and putting in order their own miserable dwellings ... their parents being obliged to keep open house to receive them at night could no longer resort to vagrancy, which they willingly gave up' (Watson, 1876). Local working people, in Aberdeen at least, subscribed to the schools because, they said (Watson, 1880), 'formerly the poor neglected children earning a living by begging led ours astray'. Watson was totally opposed to harsh repressive measures and to the traditional idea that liberal relief led to pauperisation. Yet he was also opposed to extravagance and spoke out against money being mis-spent on status symbols to glorify the benefactor as, he claimed, was the case with some orphanages. He believed that 'all giving to the poor should proceed from a principle of benevolence' and that this could only be achieved by 'house to house visitation to ascertain who are poor and not in receipt of paupers relief ... And it is held that the poor are not pauperised by the relief thus afforded' (Watson, 1876).

Watson was an able propagandist and some of his ideas spread so that in a few years, in the 1840s, industrial feeding schools were started in the major Scottish cities. He also wrote pamphlets on unemployment and illegitimacy (examining statistics to see whether there was a relationship between the two), and he was concerned with working-class conditions in the country as well as in the towns. He had opposition; on the one hand from some Parochial Boards and on the other hand from traditional charitable interests. In 1852 a rival school was started based on the premise that 'improvidence and intemperance are the chief causes of poverty and pauperism' (Watson, 1876)!

Watson had visited Owen's factory at New Lanark and had met both Mary Carpenter and Elizabeth Fry. One of Fry's helpers, Elizabeth Ogilvie worked closely with Watson, setting up the first industrial feeding school for girls in Aberdeen (Angus, 1913).

The leading individuals engaged in direct social action (of whom we have selected four) maintained some contact with one another through conferences and meetings of the Social Science Association in the 1850s and 1860s. Yet they never constituted a coherent movement in the sense that the cos represented a movement. Each of the personalities we have considered had his or her own admirers and followers: 'Owenites', 'Fry Visitors', and so on. Their individualistic schemes, furthermore, did not long remain in the form of their founder's image if, indeed, in the case of Owen, they remained at all. Yet these people were all great innovators, leaders in the realm of practical ideals which, in later generations, re-emerged in modified, partial and more permanent forms. Apart from the well-known Owenite derivatives in the co-operative movement, Owenite ideas (indirectly) influenced the neighbourhood educational work of Octavia Hill and the Settlement movement. Fry's ideas may have had only limited influence on the development of the penal system (Kent, 1962). But her emphasis on sympathetic listening became part of a tradition which, perhaps, considerably influenced later social work practice. The ideas of Carpenter and Watson influenced the subsequent development of approved schools. Sadly, in his own lifetime, most of Watson's schools became residential as a condition of receiving government aid, but the link between home and school was retained in the Scottish Approved School system through the use of social workers employed on the residential staff until, with the Social Work (Scotland) Act 1968, the responsibility passed to local authority social work departments.

The general significance of direct social action for social

work is, perhaps, threefold. First, its insistence on personal involvement modified, and romanticised, the tendency to detached investigation associated with the Charity Organisation Society. Second, its broad focus on society as well as on the individual promoted the idea of the indivisibility of social needs which later particularly influenced neighbourhood and community work. Third, it emphasised a rejection of social violence as a method of social action and a belief in social education.

The three forms of social action we have considered: social action in social administration, the charity organisation movement and direct social action, to some extent have their counterparts today, as a residue of past traditions. The tradition of innovation within government social service is illustrated, for example, in enlightened experiments in therapeutic communities both in the hospital and in the penal services. Part of the cos tradition still rests with the Family Welfare Association although, today, there may be less emphasis on poverty, and the scale and claims of the cos as a movement are much reduced. There is a revived interest in direct social action and some modern counterparts of those we have considered would be David Wills, Des Wilson, or Group Captain Cheshire, to name just a few.

However, these three forms of social action are less important as separate identifiable traditions in relation to social work now than they are, combined and fused, in relation to the emergence of social work at the end of the nineteenth and the beginning of the twentieth centuries. Social action within social administration provided organisational precedent and stability; the charity organisation movement provided the tradition of investigation, individualisation and the elements of professional training; direct social action provided the involvement, social evangelism, social pacifism, romanticism and breadth of vision. Social work contained all these ingredients.

27

Of those whose work we have described in this chapter, perhaps William Watson should have a more prominent place in social work history than he has usually been accorded. We are therefore ending this chapter with a piece of case material published in 1851 to raise support for the industrial feeding schools. It illustrates Watson's central belief in the interdependence of educational institutions and the home environment (1851):

The surviving parent is a widow; she has an only son; family affliction and family bereavement have brought her very low. She has yielded to the pressure of calamity, and bending, as she terms it, to the stroke of fate, yields herself up to gloomy despair. Her son is still an object of interest, but he is active, intelligent and self-willed. Seduced by vicious associates, he is led from one act of criminality to another, till at last he is convicted and imprisoned. This seems to set the seal on the mother's evil destiny. Shame is added to despondency and she sits alone bemoaning her unhappy lot.

The term of her son's imprisonment has expired. He has been admitted to the industrial feeding school. There he has found everything to interest and exercise for every faculty; his energies are excited, his understanding improved, his manners cultivated, his good dispositions stimulated, and his bad subdued.

His mother's drooping interest in her son revives. Assured of his safety she passes the day in comparative content. She looks for his return at night with pleasure. Her morbid feelings disappear; she must make her son's bed; and must waken him in the morning and prepare him for school. She hears the neighbours praise his activity, his intelligence and his good looks, and a mother's pride springs up in her breast. She has now a duty to perform and she rouses herself up to the task. It is a pleasing one, and the pleasure repays the labour of the performance.

She forgets that sorrow and care once afflicted her, and she blesses the day when her son entered the Industrial School.

28

3

The origins of social work
as a social movement

Among those who formed a bridge between the three
forms of social action we considered in the last chapter,
two are particularly important in the development of
social work, Octavia Hill and Canon Barnett. We will first
examine the forms of social action with which they are
associated and then see how social work developed in a
particular social context.

Octavia Hill

Octavia Hill, like Mary Carpenter, was brought up as a
Unitarian. She is important partly because of the sheer
length of her extremely active life beginning when, aged
fourteen, she was put in charge of a co-operative business
employing ragged school children to make toy furniture
in 1853. Apart from some periods of ill-health (which she
spent in the Lake District getting new ideas about the
importance of open spaces!) she was active in a wide
range of connected activities until her death in 1912.

Octavia Hill is also important because during this time
she became fully identified with the charity organisation
movement (being a member of the central committee of
the cos from 1875) and, at the same time, no less associated with the traditions and practice of direct social action.

This point tends to get lost in assessments of her work. Social work writers, from Mary Richmond (1915) onwards, have stressed her role within the COS and in promoting professional training. Other writers, outside social work (Owen, 1965) have stressed her role as a social reformer in connection with housing improvement or in connection with open spaces and the founding of the National Trust. The crucial point about her work, however, is that these two roles were interdependent. The one was meaningless to her without the other. Whereas her grandfather, Dr Southwood Smith (who, together with her Christian Socialist mother, brought her up) may have walked a tightrope as a social administrator, with Chadwick, in the public health movement between saying whether character or social conditions were responsible for poverty, Octavia Hill insisted that it was both. Poverty was due both to individual and to societal deficiency. People and their environment needed to be changed. She was prepared to hunt with the hounds of the COS to investigate thoroughly personal circumstances and yet, at the same time, to run with the hares of direct social action to recast society in magnificent images inspired, at one stage, by John Ruskin who was himself most of all influenced by the ideas of Robert Owen.

Like Owen, Octavia Hill was only to a limited extent interested in legislative reforms, for example, to promote open spaces and to protect housing standards. The idea of a state system of social insurance appalled her. The reason was not that she was politically conservative, or reactionary, as Beatrice Webb (1948) believed, but that she was committed to social change by other methods, in keeping with the traditions of direct social action. These were to re-activate a sense of mutual obligation in society through a process of neighbourhood education. She was, as R. H. Tawney (1964) said of Robert Owen, 'haunted by the associations of the term community'. Thus, when asked why she opposed statutory social insurance, she replied (Bell,

1942): 'If you desire to equalise incomes, I should advise you to do it by giving liberal wages, arranging for reasonable hours of work, and taking a large view of your duties to all men ... not by giving from a compulsory tax upon your poor neighbour as well as on yourself.'

Octavia Hill set an example in practice in her own role as landlord. Landlord and tenant, she believed, had mutual obligations. In fulfilling these obligations, on what she termed a 'human' basis, happiness and beauty could be created in the community. Rents, like wages, had to be 'fair' and not simply based on supply and demand. But this being the case, they had to be paid. At the end of the day she believed, as Owen had believed at New Lanark, a profit of 5 per cent interest on capital should be shown and, then, the balance should be either ploughed back in improvements or returned to the tenants in the form of reduced rents. (The money was lent by Ruskin and both agreed that 5 per cent was a fair rent. Ruskin, characteristically, regarded the scheme as entirely his own, and does not mention Octavia Hill in his own account of it.)

Management, education, friendship and social action were all parts of Octavia Hill's neighbourhood task. It involved a variety of schemes: inducing tenants to take more responsibility for repairs, persuading them to rent extra rooms when they could afford it to avoid overcrowding, introducing ideas about open spaces and play areas, starting play groups, mothers' groups and, in one instance, a fathers' group, and, as the base activity, maintaining regular home visiting. As her schemes grew (at one time she was responsible for more than 100,000 dwellings) she employed many helpers and, in her later years, placed increasing emphasis on training. Her ideas about training in turn influenced both the Settlement movement and the development of training within the COS.

It is hardly surprising that Octavia Hill should have been attracted to certain aspects of the Settlement movement

31

started in 1884 when Canon Barnett became Warden of Toynbee Hall. Octavia Hill's particular interest was later in connection with Nelson Sq. Settlement in Southwark.

Samuel Barnett

Canon Samuel Barnett is the second example of those who formed an important bridge between the three forms of social action we considered in the last chapter. His philosophy and practice typified direct social action. He was also attracted to certain features of the charity organisation movement, in particular the insistence of individualising social problems, or, as he put it, 'one by one', which was a kind of slogan for Toynbee Hall. Although he left the committee of the cos in disagreement over policy about social insurance he remained a vice-president. Equally important, Barnett retained close ties with the traditions of social administration and was himself for thirty years a member of the Whitechapel Board of Guardians. In general, he was much more politically conscious than Octavia Hill, but the political process was, for both of them, secondary to the educational process.

Toynbee Hall and the Settlement movement

The Settlement idea specifically originated in a letter Barnett (1915) wrote suggesting that 'men might hire a house, where they could come for short or long periods, and, living in an industrial quarter, learn to sup sorrows with the poor ... Close personal knowledge of individuals among the poor must precede wise legislation for remedying their needs.' The original objects were formally stated as follows:

(a) To provide education and the means of recreation and enjoyment for the people of the poor districts of London and other great cities;

(b) To enquire into the condition of the poor, and to consider and advance plans calculated to promote their welfare.

The range of Settlement activities is summarised in an early pamphlet written by Barnett (1896):

> Each resident takes up some citizen's duty which brings him into contact with others and puts him into a position both to learn and to teach. The aim of all, whether they serve on public boards or in clubs, whether they take part in social movements or teach classes, whether they organise lectures or entertainment, whether they become school managers or children's playmates, whether they serve on committees or personally visit the poor, whether they preach the gospel or serve human needs, is first to form friendships and then through friendship to raise the standard of living and of life.

Barnett's own position as a social pacifist was explicit. He abhorred punishment and violence and was obsessed with education (Barnett, 1915): 'The Tower of London would be a better defence for the nation if it were a centre for teaching, than as a barracks for soldiers.' More seriously, his attitude to social change in 1905 is summed up as follows (Barnett, 1915):

> Reformers may today pass laws which would exalt the poor and bring down the rich, but if, in the process of such laws, bitterness, anger or uncharitableness were increased and if, as a result, the exalted poor proved incapable of using or enjoying their power—another giant behaving like a giant—where would be the world's gain?

The dock strike of 1889 forced Toynbee Hall to clarify its attitude to industrial direct action. The facilities of Toynbee Hall were made available to the strike leaders, residents formed a strike relief committee, and there was a celebration supper at Toynbee Hall after the event. Yet, for Barnett, the whole business was foremost an educational rather than a political exercise, and, in a speech, 'Mr Barnett stated ... the settlement could not be identified with the strike nor with the party of September 21st to celebrate its successful issue' (*Toynbee Record*, 1889).

Toynbee Hall served as a laboratory for testing principles of social action which, in the last years of the nineteenth century, came to be identified with social work. We will now, very briefly, consider the social context of the period.

Towards the end of the nineteenth century, a social reckoning began to take place. The images and assumptions associated with the Victorian era were questioned. Was social progress as real as scientific progress? How real was prosperity when large sections of the population were shown to be living in poverty? From such questioning there developed an awareness of, and interest in, identifying and solving social problems.

A developing social consciousness

There were four facets to this developing social consciousness which particularly related to the origins of social work. First, in relation to the degree of social ignorance, how much did the middle classes really know about working-class conditions? Second, there was concern about the size of some of the problems creating social distress. In sheer numbers, there were more elderly and handicapped people in need of attention. There was awareness of the large numbers of families in poverty through sickness or unemployment; of the welfare needs of children (exposed through the introduction of compulsory elementary education) and of the educational needs of adults. Third, there was realisation of the limited part philanthropy could play in solving these problems and of the inevitability of some forms of statutory provision, however limited. Fourth, there was an awareness of the growing confidence of the working classes in organising their own forms of self-help. Philanthropists as well as politicians had to take this into account. Throughout the nineteenth century the poor had been exhorted to be thrifty and to help themselves. Their success in so doing was now evident in the co-operative societies, mutual aid and benefit societies and workers' educational associations, as well as in trade unions.

In this situation, the Settlement idea rapidly spread although Barnett avoided trying to stamp his own methods on other Settlements and a wide variety of institutions developed under the Settlement umbrella. Within a number of these Settlements a sense of excitement grew around the belief that they had stumbled on a key to new methods of social advance. This was expressed, for example, by Sir Walter Besant in the inaugural address at the opening of Mansfield House new residence, on 5 December 1897 (Reason, 1898):

> Though there have been many men and women devoted to humanitarian work of different kinds—sporadic cases such as those of Raikes, of Buxton, of Elizabeth Fry—there has been no large organisation, such as that of the Franciscans, in the direction of personal devotion.
>
> We have attempted other forms of philanthropic endeavour; enormous sums—millions upon millions have been given in charity. In spite of all, there has been little improvement; the slums seem to grow only worse instead of better, until—when? where? how?—we know not; but, suddenly, as it seemed, unexpected as we thought, there ran through the minds of men and women the same words, the same formula, at the same time—'Not money, but yourselves' ...
>
> The note of new philanthropy is personal service ... not a subscription, not speeches on a platform; not tracts; not articles in Quarterly Reviews; none of the old methods: but personal service.

He goes on to speak of the debt to past writers, including

35

Carlyle, Browning, Toynbee and to that which was 'plainly taught by Ruskin'.

In describing the principles of this 'new philanthropy' we find other writers using the term 'social work'. For example, Arthur Sherwell emphasises that social work must be rooted in sound knowledge (Reason, 1898):

> Facts challenge questions far more powerfully than theories and the best service that the friends of social progress can render to the cause of reform today is patiently and dispassionately to investigate and to disclose the actual facts of our existing social life ... It is not that the community is either callous or unjust. It is merely ignorance. It waits to be convinced; and conviction can only spring from Knowledge.
>
> The first and most important business therefore that lies before the social worker is to organise the instruments of knowledge.

The same writer goes on to define the relationship of social work to politics:

> The social worker, it must be remembered, holds a brief not for a class, but for a principle of justice and right dealing, in the light of which he is called upon to examine the facts and to give help and sympathy.
>
> The moral necessities of the case will often compel him to take sides, and to take sides fearlessly, in particular controversies or disputes, but he must not choose his side impulsively, nor by an invariable principle of partisanship, or his influence will assuredly be minimised, and his social usefulness in the larger possibilities destroyed.

Early examples of social work

In practical terms, the kinds of work to which these principles applied took various forms. Sometimes the focus was specific, such as in the Tenants' Protection Committee in East London in 1899, associated with Toynbee Hall, 'to combat cases of actual illegality where helpless and ignorant tenants are impressed by unscrupulous landlords' (*Annual Report*, 1899). Professional legal advice was obtained and many cases were taken to court. Sometimes the focus was more general: for example, the focus of a 'neighbourhood guild', at Allcroft Road in north-west London was described (Reason, 1898) as starting with the idea

> that all the people in any one street, or any small number of streets, in every working class district of London shall be organised into a set of clubs which are, by themselves, or in alliance with those of another neighbourhood, to carry out, or induce others to carry out all the reforms—domestic, industrial, educational, provident or recreational—which the social ideal demands.

Sometimes social work was concerned with the large-scale organisation of recreational and educational activities such as day outings and country holidays for children; and sometimes it was concerned with a modest experimental project. For example, what we would nowadays call a day centre for handicapped children was started as a school for cripples, associated with the Women's Settlement in Canning Town: 'The children are collected by means of a donkey carriage' (Reason, 1898). An early reference to the term social work is in connection with the founding of Lancashire College Settlement in Manchester, in 1895, described as 'the outcome of social work on the part of the students and friends of Lancashire [Congregationalist] College' (Reason, 1898), but it is not specified what the social work was. And so on. There are many examples of these sorts of activities at the end of the nineteenth century, in addition to the older tradition of charity visiting within a neighbourhood, which were seen as parts of a social mission to understand and to influence the social environment through personal intervention, in the spirit of 'not money, but yourselves'.

Social work as a movement, however, found its most clear sense of identity in activities directed towards the promotion of training. At the end of the nineteenth century the COS was turning its attention increasingly towards training, not only in the narrow sense of training charity workers in casework, but in relation to the wider aspects of what the COS called 'propagandism', that is to say the spread of charitable principles. A Joint Lectures Committee (linking central and local COS interests and also representatives from the Women's University Settlement, Southwark) was founded in 1896, with a full-time lecturer. Its first Annual Report (quoted in the 14th COS *Annual Report*) said:

> No opportunity should be lost for emphasising the organising side of casework and the importance of influencing local relief work ... They [volunteers] should be encouraged to join parish relief committees, boards of managements of hospitals, dispensaries, Boards of Guardians, to become School Board Managers ... The first object of anyone who is trained himself would be to help to train others.

Training was soon linked with the desire to 'think big' within the COS as within the Settlements. 'It is no longer the day of very small things,' says the COS *Annual Report* of 1898, 'such as will never be known beyond a few garrets and workshops. Instead of this it is the desire of many to make a new era.'

The COS, however, conceded that it could not make a new era without some outside support, and in 1901, 'after much deliberation and consultation' the links between the COS and the Settlement movement (and through the Settlements with the Universities) broadened. An initiative was taken in the form of a circular addressed to those in the Universities, the COS and Settlements who were interested in 'social and economic work', and this led to the establishment of full-time courses in social studies or sociology

which, combined with practical work, constituted professional training for social work. The first of these courses,
on a full-time basis, was established in a specially founded
School of Sociology in Southwark, in a ferment of social
evangelism. The tutor, E. J. Urwick, wrote at the time
(Loch, 1904):

> The trained workers of today must be more than mere
> administrators; they must be the apostles of true doc-
> trines, and they must preach in the language of their
> generation ... The terms in which our truths are ex-
> pressed often belong to a past age; have we not all been
> at times uneasily conscious that the mere appeal
> to fundamental principles of self-help, independence,
> thrift and the like, has lost much of its force, and that
> these principles must be re-cast ... Within the last
> decade a new science has come to the front—the science
> of social life, of sociology ... This movement (for it
> deserves the name) offers the opportunity we want.

Urwick seems to use the term 'sociology' ambiguously,
since he goes on to say that the academic curriculum for
social workers *included* sociology, social psychology,
social economics and history. The term 'sociology' in the
context of a movement covers all these subjects as dis-
ciplines. As regards practical work, Urwick says (Loch,
1904):

> The student must study the concrete material to be
> found in existing social conditions. It is doubtful
> whether this can be done by simple observation. At any
> rate it will be better done, and without danger, if he
> is set to work in some of the simplified and more natural
> (i.e. non-patronising) ways under the guidance of an
> experienced administrator or social worker.

As a social movement, social work sought to distinguish itself from political movements on the one hand, and
from religious movements on the other hand. Social work
was differentiated from politics in so far as it was less

interested in the distribution of power than in the resolution of social conflict. Its goal was a social ideal, not a
political system. As such, it was seen by its exponents
as something better than purely political activity—in
Barnett's words 'a sort of progress whose means would
justify the end'.

The differentiation of social work from religious movements was not always clear. In the Settlements, in particular, the social gospel was sometimes entangled with
the religious gospel. The cos solved this problem by seeing
itself as an alternative to religious evangelism. Charity
was the fruit of true religious faith and, as Loch (1904) put
it, 'in fervency it is religious'.

During its first phase of development, social work lacked
specific organisational forms with which its adherents
could be associated, and automatically by such association,
claim to be 'social workers'. Identification with social work
derived from the sense of belonging to a general social
movement which linked the interests of those engaged in
specific activities within various organisations. Each of
these organisations continued to have its own traditions,
specific objectives, and terminology. The unity of purpose
of social work expressed itself chiefly in relation to the
need for training. Education was a means of sustaining
and disciplining a social mission which otherwise might
be deflected into uniformed political, religious, or philanthropic activities. Yet this unity covered up important
ideological differences within the social work movement.
These became polarised in attitudes to the work of the
Poor Law Commission established in 1905 and which
reported in 1909, separately as the majority and the
minority. (In general the cos supported the majority view,
while views within the Settlement movement varied.)

Social work as a movement spread rapidly in the early
years of the twentieth century throughout the country and
abroad, until the outbreak of the First World War. This
marked the end of the period of social evangelism in

which social work originated. To the romantic social pacifists steeped in the traditions of direct social action with
its central beliefs in the rationality of man and the possibility of human betterment through education, the First
World War came as a shock and represented failure and
disillusionment. In terms of manpower its effects were
also disruptive. The war situation, it is true, also presented fresh challenges. These were taken up through
fresh organisations, and in particular through the movement which led, after the war, to the creation of the
National Council of Social Service (Kuenstler, 1961). But
the original, heroic phase associated with the origins of
social work as a social movement had passed.

4

Social work—movement or profession?

While social work was establishing itself as a social movement, certain kinds of activities within the movement were becoming professionalised. In this chapter we consider very briefly the conflict of objectives between social work as a movement and social work as a profession.

We saw in the last chapter that social work found its identity most clearly in relation to the promotion of social work education. But what was this education for? Was it intended that the knowledge gained was to be passed on to volunteers so that they would become more effective in spreading the beliefs of social work as a social movement? Or was it to provide expertise in relation to professional areas of practice from which the volunteer was excluded? Or was it, somehow, a combination of the two?

The answers to these questions varied, even within the COS. This is illustrated in relation to the beginnings of almoning. The first paid almoner (in Britain) was jointly appointed by the COS and the Royal Free Hospital in 1895. The arrangement was originally entered into by the COS in a spirit of seizing an opportunity to propagate charitable principles. Thus 'almonership' was described as 'all that charity can suggest' in solving the problems of an overcrowded out-patients and casualty department. (From the hospital board's point of view it may have appealed more as a practical means of preventing the abuse of free services.) However, early reports to the cos also express apprehension about the possibility of appointing untrained almoners (cos, *Annual Report*, 1899, 1900).

The gap between the professional and the volunteer

The professionalisation of social work must be understood in the context of a general move in the direction of professionalisation amongst teachers, nurses and other groups. In order to be effective, the almoner wanted to show other professionals that she was competent in relation to certain areas of practice and entitled by virtue of training and experience to make professional judgments. This inevitably tended to produce a gap between the professional and the volunteer social worker who lacked training. Originally, as we saw in the last chapter, to be 'trained' meant 'trained' to instruct volunteers as, for example, in the case of cos secretaries. Subsequently, the professional worker took over certain duties from which the volunteer was excluded and, by stages, this led eventually to the extraordinary position held by one group of professional workers giving evidence to the Aves (1969) Committee: 'The feeling was that voluntary workers could be useful if we only had time to cope with them. The conclusion was that this was a vicious circle—we have not time to organise volunteers, so we run around doing the work ourselves.' The emphasis had thus changed from training volunteers to excluding them from professional practice, and, in time, groups of volunteers came to be organised separately (for example, within Councils of Social Service), from the various professional groups of social workers practising in probation, almoning, the cos and, later, in psychiatric social work.

Yet the sense of social mission was not entirely lost within professional groups. To some extent the conflict

43

between the objectives of the movement and the objectives of the profession was resolved by stressing 'casework principles'. These principles were derived from the principles of social action which guided the early social work movement—the 'friendship' which was the basis of settlement work, of Octavia Hill's 'human work' (as she called it), and which Loch also countenanced within the concept of 'charity'—and these ideas were not so much discarded as professionalism occurred but were re-phrased, developed, refined, and made to appear scientific in influential American literature; for example, in Mary Richmond's (1915) ideas about 'diagnosis' and 'treatment'. (Father Biestek (1957), much later, even argued that through the medium of the 'casework relationship' the social worker could be identified with 'divine providence'.) Casework principles were not confined to social work with clients. Mary Richmond's 'indirect' work, in one sense, meant retaining a sense of mission in dealing with other agents in order to help the client. And she also recognised that social casework had to go hand in hand with social reform.

The effect of professionalisation in Britain, however, was to fragment social work in terms of specialisms which came to be identified with particular settings. Such fragmentation was closely related to administrative fragmentation within the piecemeal development of social services, during the period up to 1939. Whereas in the Settlements and in Octavia Hill's work, working with individuals had not been differentiated as a separate kind of activity from working with groups or with communities, professionalisation, combined with administrative developments, separated such activities. Work with individuals as clients, was in general associated with health services. Professional social workers, as caseworkers, evolved a group of concepts mainly borrowed from medicine (like 'diagnosis') and, later, from psychoanalysis. Work with groups and communities, on the other hand, was more closely related to educational interests, and followed a very differ-

44

ent path of professional progress associated, for example, with the youth and community service. To some extent social studies courses held these two groups together (and also personnel management), but such courses were eventually regarded as only 'basic' so far as 'professional specialisms' (for example, psychiatric social work) was concerned.

In spite of the fragmentation of social work, the vague idea that social work was a general social movement persisted, both within and outside activities which became professionalised. This, no doubt, was possibly due to the lack of clear definition of the objectives of the movement. Settlements, in particular, showed a remarkable resilience. Between the two world wars some of them turned their attention to problems created by unemployment, and new educational Settlements were founded. Social work as a movement still influenced the processes of professionalisation in drawing together social workers in different fields. The British Federation of Social Workers, in the 1930s, was not solely concerned with the promotion of professional interests but took an interest in social action.

In general, however, while the movement still persisted between the wars, it was a pale shadow of the old movement at the end of the nineteenth century, with its vast claim then to the formula for social advance. The prescription 'not money, but yourselves' was no more helpful to the millions of unemployed than was psychoanalytic theory which was beginning to affect casework. The hopes of those who wished to see a better society turned to political movements. By 1939 social work as a movement was eclipsed, as a profession fragmented and as practice uninspiring.

PART II

Family casework
and the welfare state bureaucracy

5

Social work and the arrival of the welfare state

The argument in Part I, in which we were concerned with the first phase of the expansion of social work in Britain, can be summarised as follows. Social work came into being at the end of the nineteenth century at a time of social reckoning to replace traditional ideas about the role of philanthropy in relation to the solution of social problems. The philanthropic answer to social problems had consisted in a charitable transaction between the rich and the poor. This tradition preceded and accompanied the Industrial Revolution. Within the context of the general philanthropic response to large-scale social distress in the nineteenth century, three particular disciplined forms of social action developed which questioned the traditional tenets of the charitable transaction. It was from a fusion of these forms of social action that the particular principles and practices which characterised social work emerged. The three forms of disciplined social action were: first, social action within the tradition of professional social administration; second, social action within the charity organisation movement; and, third, a romantic individualistic tradition based on principles of social pacifism which we have called 'direct social action'. Each of these three forms of social action emphasised the role of social education and it was in this context that social work as a movement gave birth to social work as a profession. The movement stood for the application of scientific principles and humanitarian philosophy to an understanding and a solution of social problems.

Social work, however, was only one of the products of the period of social reckoning to which we have referred. Another product, of greater importance, was the application of a new political philosophy, based on what the Webbs called 'the household state', which began to be constructed shortly after social work as a movement emerged, and about which social workers were ideologically divided. In small stages, between the world wars, the construction of the household state continued while social work as a movement was increasingly eclipsed. After the war, a comprehensive system of statutory social services was finally constructed on the basis and plan of what came to be known as the welfare state.

In Part II we shall be examining the expansion of social work in an entirely different context from that in which social work began. Nevertheless it is a context in which the original question we asked about the role of philanthropy and charity in society can be asked again in relation to the role of social work. In Part I we saw that the charitable transaction fulfilled the function of over-simplifying social conflict and thus sustaining the ideal images associated with the consolidation of established national institutions. In Part II we shall be looking at the symbolic role of social work, and, in particular of family casework, in relation to the problems associated with the need to personalise systems of social service.

1945 marks the final establishment in Britain of the national state, as entrusted by popular consent with powers over the individual citizen in peace time previously only equalled in wartime. The powers were commensurate with the expectations. The state was entrusted to introduce and to sustain, through the enactment and embodiment of the sentiment of welfare, that universal harmony of social interest which philanthropists in the nineteenth century had vainly striven for through voluntary effort. We shall be examining how social work found a new social role in relation to this sentiment, this image. We shall see that this was not, in the period which we are now considering, in terms of reconciling conflicting social and class interests, but in terms of reconciling the individual and the state. Traditionally, the charitable transaction had hidden uncomfortable realities about social conflicts in a situation of social upheaval. In the 1950s, uncomfortable realities about deficiencies in the welfare state and in its structure were hidden through a new kind of role-play, this time between the social worker and the deviant client. The new role-play was, however, only a variation on the old charitable transaction between the philanthropist and the pauper. Whereas the pauper in the nineteenth century was essentially the person who could be *seen*, visibly, not to be benefiting from the *laissez faire* system of capitalism, and its accompanying idealised imagery of prosperity and of progress so, too, in the 1950s, the deviant was essentially the person who could be *seen* not to be benefiting from the beneficent power of the welfare state. To his rescue, or to effect his control, came various forms of social work.

The meaning of the welfare state

The term 'welfare state' is said to have been coined by the Archbishop of Canterbury in 1941 in a book *Citizens and Churchmen* although, as Richard Titmuss (Schottland, 1967) points out, the term was not in widespread popular use in Britain until the early 1950s. The context of its origin, however, is significant. Political power had to be harnessed for human welfare with the same moral force with which it was harnessed to the prosecution of war, if that war was to be justified. The welfare state, in this sense, was the ideal worth fighting for. The term did not describe a state of affairs which existed but a state of affairs which many people were determined *should* exist. This is illustrated in the inspiration which came from William Beveridge's symbolic image of the Five Giants (1942):

> Now, when the war is abolishing landmarks of every kind, is the opportunity ... a revolutionary moment in the world's history ... a time for revolutions not for patching ... The organisation of social insurance should be treated as one part only of a comprehensive policy of social progress ... It is an attack upon Want. Want is only one of five Giants on the road of reconstruction and in some ways the easiest to attack. The others are Disease, Ignorance, Squalor and Idleness.

The concept of the welfare state idealised both specific systems of social welfare provision and the institution of the state itself as the provider of welfare. The principal systems of provision were those of social security and pensions, the National Health service, education, family allowances, child care, housing and planning, and national assistance. These systems justified the continued exercise of many wartime controls, including price controls and rationing, and even an extension of state powers in the National Health service and, indirectly, through a programme of nationalisation.

The place of social work

How did these idealised systems of social service provision introduced between 1944 and 1950 affect people's perception of the role of social work? There were two extreme and opposite answers depending on the way the question was put and to whom it was put. First, the question could be put: 'Does the welfare state make social work redundant?' Many socialists argued that statutory provisions expressed and embodied the principles of social justice and social concern upon which, in the nineteenth century, much voluntary action had been founded, and therefore they were not concerned with social work, which, by implication, was now all but redundant. G. D. H. Cole, in his *Intelligent Man's Guide to the Post-War World* (1947) does not even mention social work. It was conceded that voluntary social services might still fill gaps in provision, experiment with new forms of help which the state might later take over, and run certain services on behalf of the state (e.g. services for the deaf or the blind) until, eventually, statutory services might extend into virtually all fields.

On the other hand, and at the other extreme, it was possible to argue that social work in general, and social casework in particular, embodied social values which should underpin social service provision and which, more than ever, it was necessary to emphasize in the age of statutory welfare. Bureaucratic services had to be humanised, lest power through bureaucracy should become an end in itself and service systems increasingly out of touch with the needs of the individual. Social service provision required not only centralised planning but personalised delivery. As T. H. Marshall has pointed out (Morgan, 1966) the welfare state implied the ending of the traditional 'barrier of shame' associated with asking for help. 'Modern welfare policy set itself to breach the barrier of shame and replace it by the bridge of sympathy ... Hence the importance of the rehabilitation of the neighbourhood and its extension to the principle of common citizenship to include the whole community.' Such arguments might extend the role of the social worker into the sensitive area of matching community needs and services.

Among those who conceptualised the role of social work in terms of a positive relationship between state and community were social work educators of the time. For example, Cormack and MacDougal, in Morris (1949):

> The basis of all casework is the natural human response
> of one individual to another in social need which he
> cannot meet alone. Casework makes a very urgent claim
> at this juncture of affairs ... on the attentions of all
> engaged or concerned for social service. In a demo-
> cratic society casework principles must be embodied
> in the structure of these services [and] the social system
> of comprehensive general social service will need to be
> supplemented by more intensive selective casework pro-
> vision.

Social work educators were anxious to throw off the
'Lady Bountiful' image and to draw, instead, on professional
images of social work, especially those from abroad in the
United States. It is, however, possible to put too much
emphasis on the effective influence of American casework
theory on actual practice in Britain, as distinct from the
image of practice. It would seem likely that a less widely
acknowledged source of influence on post-war social work
practice in Britain, and on post-war claims for the broad
scope of social casework in relation to the welfare state,
came still from the Settlement movement and, in some
cases, from Councils of Social Service. Although, in the
post-war period, Settlements were thought to be of declin-
ing importance, in so far as some of their activities were
taken over by the state, they were still influential in
relation to social work training. Settlement wardens were
sometimes social work tutors. Most students on basic social
studies courses at this time either had one placement
in a Settlement or lived in a Settlement as a resident
for part of the time of their training. The Settlement
movement—and that of the Councils of Social Service—
appealed to the broader social purposes of social work and
this emphasis was combined in social work education
with an insistence that modern casework was now professionally and scientifically based—the evidence for
which was drawn from the United States. Thus, for example, in writing about the social studies course at Bir-

mingham University, which had been founded in 1905, the Chairman of the course wrote about 1950 (Cavenagh): 'When the course was started, social work was somewhat amateurish, and social workers were largely of the unpaid, untrained, Lady Bountiful type; now they are a selected and professionally qualified corps without whom the welfare state—and most voluntary societies—would probably be unworkable.'

It is important to distinguish the American and British traditions from which, together, the social worker's claim in relation to the welfare state derived its ideology. In America, the social services were not generally available through statutory machinery and the welfare state was a term of derision. American casework theorists appealed to general philosophical notions about the basis of a free society for their frame of reference for social work objectives. For example, Hamilton (1940): 'Social work rests ultimately on certain assumptions which cannot be proved, e.g. human betterment is the goal of any society.' In contrast, the social context of social work in Britain was more specific. The state had certain statutorily defined social duties. The role of social work was to enable these duties to be effectively performed in ways which matched personal needs. British social work educators at this time concentrated exclusively on casework theory, enriched from America, and regarded it as applicable to a wide range of settings in the British context. A report on the training of social workers produced by Eileen Younghusband in 1947 included (amazingly as it seems even since the publication of the Seebohm Committee Report in 1968) the following list of 'forms of social work' (Younghusband, 1947): almoning, child care, church work, colonial social welfare, community centre and Settlement work, community organisation, family casework, information and advice services, moral welfare, personnel management, work with the physically and mentally handicapped, probation and other services connected with the penal system,

55

psychiatric social work, youth leadership, and social work in the civil service. To this remarkable list, the report of the Birmingham Social Studies Course (to which reference has already been made in Cavenagh) added: housing managers, housemasters and housemistresses in Approved Schools, and social survey investigators.

There was at this time an extraordinary discrepancy between the theory of methods, based almost exclusively on casework theory derived from a narrow range of experience, and social work tasks which were defined in terms even broader than they are defined today. The discrepancy was reconciled by insisting that the casework relationship provided the key to the problem of humanising bureaucracy in all social institutions and in matching needs and services. This claim probably derived in no small measure from the traditional anti-bureaucratic stance of the voluntary social services in general, and the Settlement movement in particular, expressed in the slogan of Toynbee Hall, 'one by one', and in many of Barnett's writings where he expressed 'distrust of machinery': 'Men were asking for some other way than that of institutions by which to reach their neighbours' (Reason, 1898). Barnett, on the other hand, also believed that a state, so humanised, could take over the role of voluntary charity (1915): 'Charities have looked, and do look ... to their own extinction when the state, guided by their example, may take up their work.' The idea of 'one by one' was re-inforced by the theoretical casework principle of the 'one *to* one' relationship. The merging of these two streams of thought—the movement aspect which was mainly British, with the professionalising influence from America—formed the basis of the social work educator's very large claims in the immediate post-war period in Britain.

In realistic terms, however, these claims were preposterous. Talk about 'a professional corps without whom the welfare state would probably be unworkable', as though such a corps existed, or could even be envisaged, bore no relation to fact at that time. Cherry Morris spoke of wartime caseworkers being appointed locally, regionally and nationally to 'key positions in health and welfare', and she went on to claim that the effect of post-war legislation was 'to extend still more the scope for case-workers and in fields yet untried' (Morris, 1949). Yet in reality, in 1940 there had only been 165 qualified psychi-atric social workers in Britain, only a proportion of whom were practising at all, and only six of whom were working, for example, with evacuees. A further ninety-two PSWs were trained during the war (Timms, 1964). The numbers of professionally trained social caseworkers in other set-tings were also small and it is ridiculous to pretend that the welfare state in any real sense 'depended' on such small numbers of supposedly key people.

Yet, as we have said earlier, in a symbolic sense, social workers *were* important in post-war Britain. In the next chapter we will examine their symbolic importance more closely in relation to family casework and the problem family.

6

The welfare state
and the problem family

Although the welfare state had its critics, criticism was chiefly limited to a kind which did not tackle real issues. Advocacy and criticism were both based on images rather than realities. Titmuss summarises the basis of criticism of the welfare state during this period as follows. It was, he said (Schottland, 1967) criticised 'as a major instrument of re-distribution of wealth from rich to poor; as a means of impoverishing the professional and middle classes; as a denial of charity and cultural excellence; as the responsible agent in undermining the virtues of thrift, individual effort, and family stability.'

The advocates of the welfare state, on the other hand, argued that it promoted greater freedom, equality of opportunity, social security, basic minimum standards and, in general, the opportunity to build a new, free, fair and prosperous society. The hope of prosperity, after the immediate post-war period of austerity, was symbolically expressed in the building of the Royal Festival Hall which was opened, together with the South Bank Exhibition and a fun-fair at Battersea Park, to commemorate the Great Exhibition of 1851!

The unreal dialogue between critics and advocates of the welfare state, based on symbols and images rather than on defined concepts, tended to sustain an over-all myth concerning the effectiveness of the political process. The dialogue failed to reveal that what was perceived as an ideal—whether good or bad—was, in reality, far from the ideal. It was, in fact, a compromise between competing political, bureaucratic and professional interests and pressures. Each legislative provision was the product of compromise and, in implementation, there were more compromises. This has since been documented, for example, by Willcocks (1967) in relation to the creation of the National Health service, by Rubenstein and Simon (1968) in relation to education policy based on the Act of 1944, by Donnison (1967) in relation to housing and planning policies, and so on. In implementation, for example, the Education Act contained provision for the raising of the school-leaving age to sixteen. This has waited nearly thirty years for implementation. Compromise proposals for a limited development of comprehensive education, envisaged in the 1944 Act, were only implemented in a purely symbolic form, and local authority proposals to extend comprehensive education were actively blocked by central government. In a similar way, the National Health Service Act of 1946 contained provision for health centres, intended to integrate the tripartite structure of hospital, practitioner and local authority health services. Only now, twenty-five years later, are these being built on any significant scale at a time when the tripartite structure itself will shortly disappear. In the 1950s only a very small number were opened, as a gesture, such as the status, purpose-built centre at Woodberry Down in Essex. Perhaps the most fundamental compromise, as well as the one least appreciated at the time, was in relation to income support policies. Family allowances, social security benefits and minimum wages were not sufficiently high to allow the social security system as a whole to operate as Beveridge had intended. The result was that Beveridge's second, reserve, 'safety-net' system of National Assistance was never used in the limited way intended. The numbers of those receiving National Assistance steadily rose. Many people depended on it permanently. This was in spite of a level of employment which was higher than Beveridge had thought possible. (Family allowances were not given for the first child on the assumption that wages would be sufficiently high to provide for the upkeep of one dependent adult and one child. Beveridge allowed for an unemployment rate of 3 per cent, whereas in the 1950s it was between 1 and 2 per cent of the registered working population.)

Such facts, however, were uncomfortable not only for the government in power, but for the opposition and for public opinion in general to recognise. The welfare state might be right or wrong, depending on one's ideology, but right or wrong it represented the fruits of victory in war; and while it might be safely criticised by conservatives as fruit that was bad for you if you ate too much, or too quickly, it was less possible to criticise the political credibility of the process which had brought it into being. To do so, perhaps, would be to risk the possibility of exposing a deeper and wider disillusionment with the fruits of victory.

Attitudes to the problem family

While basic issues about the political process were avoided in post-war Britain, attention was focused instead on a number of other issues including how to deal with individual families who visibly failed to benefit from the welfare state. These were the so-called 'problem families'—the deviants of the 1950s who, like the paupers in the nineteenth century, were in many ways the scapegoats for the unfaced fears of society and the inadequately understood deficiencies in the social and economic system. Certainly there had been a vast improvement in the general standard of living since before the war (and there was no comparison, of course, with conditions in the nineteenth century), but the widespread assumption in 1950 was that *no one* needed any longer to be poor, and few people needed even to be miserable, in the age of welfare. This, as we now know, did not square with the facts which were to some extent even then available, for example, from Rowntree and Lavers's study (1951). Although the figures showed a drop in poverty levels compared with the previous Rowntree surveys, they gave no real grounds for complacency, especially when one takes into account that York was hardly typical of conditions in large cities. Another interesting subject was the 'spiv' who, apparently, managed to live without working in the welfare state. There is an interesting similarity of attitudes to 'charity' in the early 1830s and 'social services' in the early 1950s. For example, the following was written (Gerando) in 1833:

> He has been born for *nothing*—he has been nursed for nothing ... clothed for nothing ... put out in the world for nothing ... had medicine and medical attention for nothing; he has had his children also born, nursed, clothed, fed, educated, established, and physicked for nothing ... Finally ... he has died for *nothing. He has Lived for Nothing.*

It was a sign of the times that Penelope Hall (1952) explained to her social work readers in the first edition of *The Social Services of Modern England*: 'Not every family with a multiplicity of ... problems is a problem family. It is their attitude towards their difficulties and towards those who would help them solve them which sets such families apart.' The book gives a full chapter to the subject, in contrast to the latest edition by Forder (1971), which only mentions the subject very briefly. Less mildly, a 'study' sponsored by the National Federation of Women's Institutes, *Our Towns, A Close up* (Hall, 1952), described problem families as: 'always on the edge of pauperism' (in other words, it was not possible to say that they were *poor*) and 'riddled with mental and physical defects, in and out of the courts for child neglect, a menace to the community of which the gravity is out of all proportion to their numbers.' They were 'discovered', defined, described, counted, investigated, analysed, and often penalised. Their real crime to society, however, was seldom faced up to as honestly as in one local newspaper, which reported: 'These families are like a sore thumb held downwards in front of the cheery face of the welfare state.' (This, and other references to contemporary sources, are mostly taken from 'Sleeptite Flash', the internal newsletter of Family Service Units. This particular reference comes from 'Sleeptite Flash', March/April 1960. The cutting comes from the *Bath and Wilts Chronicle*.)

Liverpool was the first town to discover that it had problem families. It was also in Liverpool that a family service was pioneered to deal with them. From the point of view of understanding the expansion of social work this is an interesting story because, at a 'micro' level, one can trace the stages described in chapter 4 in relation to the interconnection of the 'movement' and 'professional' aspects of social work at a more general level.

The approach of the health department in Liverpool to the acknowledged social problem of the problem family was more sober than that of the study sponsored by the Women's Institutes quoted earlier. According to the Deputy Medical Officer of Health, problem families were families 'presenting an abnormal amount of subnormal behaviour over long periods with a marked tendency to backsliding' (Hall, 1952). The family casework service which developed to deal with this phenomenon started with the work of Pacifist Service Units. These were groups of conscientious objectors to military service in wartime who sought a social witness to their pacifist beliefs. The early work of the Liverpool Unit was described as a 'venture in faith'. Pacifist Service Units were, in fact, undertaking relief work of a general and varied kind in several blitzed cities, but the Liverpool Unit developed a particular interest in offering personal and practical help to families and old people considered as hopeless when it came to evacuation or billeting. The faith of Pacifist Service Units was in the intrinsic worth of each individual and in the power of love, expressed in informed and practical ways and especially in personal, friendly relationships, to reach each individual. Although they were amateurs, the early PSU workers realised the need for a disciplined approach to their work, and there was an early emphasis on the sharing of experiences, as mutual education, which later became formalised as case conferences, personal supervision of staff, and in-training.

By the end of the war, other Units were operating on these lines in Manchester and in London. In 1946 the organisation published a book, *Problem Families* (Stephens, 1946), which described the primitive conditions in which the families who were visited by the Units' workers lived. This picture contrasted with the idealised view of improved working-class conditions and standards after the war. As a result of this book the work of Pacifist Service Units was much admired and more widely known. Shortly afterwards the Liverpool and Manchester Units (but not, at first, the East London Unit at Stepney) decided to identify themselves clearly as a professionally organised family casework service in co-operation with, and supplementary to, the services of the welfare state, while retaining the flexibility, team spirit and the basis of personal friendship which characterized their original approach.

Development of Family Service Units

In 1947 the name of the organisation was changed to 'Family Service Units' and under its new name the work expanded. By June 1954 forty-three casework staff were employed. Its rate of expansion, however, was limited, not by demand from local authorities, but by its own policy of carefully selecting candidates for posts. New posts were only created in relation to the rate of recruitment for existing posts. In the year ending 30 June 1953, out of 500 enquiries and 150 applications, sixty were interviewed and only thirteen appointed—in spite of the fact that no specific formal qualifications were required. Another limiting factor was finance. Although many local authorities approached FSU during the 1950s requesting the establishment of Units, with offers to provide a proportion (often 50 per cent) of the costs, voluntary sources of income were not always easily found.

FSU was an example of a voluntary organisation recognised by statutory agencies to be filling a gap in service provision and pioneering new forms of service. Clearly identified with social work, after 1947, its services for a time tended to become more specialised in the sense that they were more specifically oriented towards the provision of a casework service for selected families. Work with old people was not developed. Some Units ran clubs and holiday schemes but these were to assist families already being helped with casework. FSU tried to develop professional knowledge as a basis for practice, while retaining some of the earlier practices, such as calling clients by their Christian names, and wearing informal dress. Other wartime practices were discarded, usually slowly, such as the insistence that workers should themselves be residents in Unit Centres. This practice had originated partly on grounds of economy (living together was cheaper when no one was paid a salary), partly for reasons of morale, and perhaps partly to identify with the neighbourhood in which they worked. It was eventually dropped when it was decided, on professional grounds, that it was not necessary, or consistent with sound professional practice, to encourage families to be too dependent on the Unit— as well as because increasingly most workers preferred to live away from where they worked. Units, whether resident or non-resident, emphasised the importance of

Unit facilities for receiving and entertaining families. Facilities usually included a bathroom, kitchen, 'families room', clothing store, and provision for storing gifts of furniture, as well as office accommodation. Many Units also had a dining room, where staff lunches were eaten and visitors entertained. In terms of casework practice, there was a fairly smooth development from old to new ideas, based on an affinity of principles between pacifism as a movement and social casework as a professional method. Casework principles, read from American textbooks, reinforced, on the whole, the practices that FSU workers had discovered for themselves to be effective and intrinsically right. It was easy to substitute 'acceptance' for friendship, 'self-determination' for respect for each individual, and 'controlled expression of feelings' for sympathetic listening.

The essential characteristics of what was called 'the FSU approach', as a professional casework service, were the following. First, a restricted caseload. FSU believed that there was only point in accepting just the number of families that could be visited regularly and for as long as necessary. Families that could not be immediately accepted were kept on a waiting-list. Second, flexibility of approach and methods. Free from statutory definitions of duties, FSU workers were, in theory, able to try whatever method suited each family situation: giving material aid, sometimes regularly if self-questioningly; offering practical assistance such as decorating; organising small groups for children, mothers or occasionally fathers; regular interview sessions in the home or, less often, at the Unit Centre, or regular weekly collection of rent and other debts on behalf of creditors (a practice which has since become widespread in local authority departments). More recently some units have undertaken forms of community work, but this did not occur in the 1950s. Third, the principle of teamwork and, specifically, acceptance of the idea of staff supervision which, in FSU preceded the professional supervision of outside students. Fourth, the voluntary principle. Families were usually referred by other agencies already in touch or to whom the families presented administrative problems. The FSU worker would enter the home on an initial visit, explain the circumstances of the referral, but would dissociate himself from the interests of the referral agency and would, instead, stress the fact that FSU would only visit with the family's consent to deal with problems which they, themselves, wished to be tackled. Workers were sometimes refused entry, although this was not very common. In some Units, the general practice was for two workers to go together on the first visit. Afterwards the workers would confer before deciding whether the case should be 'accepted'. Cases which were not accepted (usually on the grounds that their problems did not appear sufficiently serious) were referred to other agencies. Fifth, the principle of considering the family as a whole. In most cases, both parents were consulted before taking a family 'on'. Finally, the anti-bureaucratic approach to Unit administration. Each member of staff shared professional and administrative duties (with the exception of secretarial staff and the housekeepers of resident Units). The 'Fieldwork Organiser' of each Unit usually carried a small case-load. In management, there was an ingenious mixture of decentralised financing, local domestic management, but centralised policies on recruitment, selection of staff, training and development. Family Service Units officially consisted of all the local units, together, plus the national committee. The national committee included representatives from local committees. Effective control, nationally, rested with a sub-committee of the national committee which included staff as well as committee members. Some committee members were also ex-members of staff, so that staff exercised considerable control over policy.

Other solutions

FSU represented the least 'tough' of several possible societal responses to the problem of how to deal with a problem family. Another possibility was residential care for the mother and her young children. This varied from a 'recuperative centre' in Cheshire, to a home for 'neglectful mothers' in York. 'Tougher' alternative proposals were plentiful. The Medical Officer of Health for Kidderminster, among others, suggested that problem families should be placed in a colony of 'simple, strong, virtually undamageable dwellings', free of rent, and 'where they must be under the direction of a residential welfare officer' who would organise 'a communal meals service' ('Sleeptite Flash', September/October 1955). The *News Chronicle* pointed out that this would amount to 'moral apartheid'. Other suggestions included the use of old dwellings, while an even tougher solution was imprisonment. Special provision was made at Winston Green Prison, Birmingham, to provide training for mothers of problem families convicted of neglecting their children or, occasionally, cruelty. Fathers could be imprisoned (in England and Wales) as the consequence of getting into debt, through failing to comply with a court order. This was a common occurrence in some areas with families known to FSU (e.g. Birmingham). Another suggested solution was sterilisation. In 1955, for example, at the Annual Conference of the Association of Hospital Management Committees, it was suggested that 'voluntary sterilisation' might prevent 'a great deal of social misery and reduce the unpleasantly high number of problem families'. Not infrequently, families were referred to FSU in the hope that the mother could be persuaded to accept sterilisation. Family planning was, of course, also suggested, but with the majority of FSU families to whom this was suggested, the attempt was futile. (The point that Engels made in describing the conditions of the working class in England in 1844 is probably applicable to the condition of problem families in 1950. What else had they to look forward to but drink and sex? They resented interference with either.)

FSU workers were frequently praised as saintly people who were prepared to work so patiently with 'hopeless cases'. The *Children's Newspaper*, in November 1955, referred to FSU as 'The Finest Job in the World'. This, of course, did not fit the professional image FSU was trying to achieve, particularly when popular publicity invariably painted the contrast between the hopelessness of the task and the dramatic action Units were supposed to take, such as scrubbing the floors or, in one case, 'living with the family'. FSU workers were saintly because they had patience for such disagreeable people that the ordinary person was not expected to have. The acceptance of such praise involved collusion with public hostility towards problem families as deviants. This, in turn, made the job of the Units more difficult.

Throughout the 1950s the problem family became increasingly significant. It even became a form of status symbol for local authorities to have services of one kind or another designated to deal with them. Newspaper headlines and reports, documented by David Jones, then National Secretary of FSU, in the Units' internal newsletter during this period, include a reference to home helps in Staffordshire getting 6d. an hour more for working with problem families, while a press cutting for 1956 announces: 'Bootle has placed the duty of supervising and visiting problem families on health visitors.' Everyone could 'have a go'. Youth leaders, probation officers, police, magistrates, doctors, all had something to contribute while health, welfare or children's departments in some areas, for example in Northumberland, developed services which were considered to be modelled on FSU methods (in some cases employing FSU personnel).

It was not realised at the time the extent to which the problem family was itself the product of the inadequacies of bureaucratic structures and services established, in some cases specially, to deal with them. Slowly, however, more attention focused on services and less on problem families. For example, at a meeting of the local Magistrates' Association in 1957, 'it was stated that a Bideford family was visited by two health visitors, two school welfare officers, two probation officers, and an NSPCC inspector. It was said that the house was flea-infested. It could also be said that it was official infested' ('Sleeptite Flash', March/April 1957).

In this context, the importance of FSU gradually broadened. It became not merely an idealised answer to the problem of the problem family and of coaxing it back into the fold of those susceptible of response to so-called normal services, but a suggestion of the possibility of a general kind of family provision, applicable not merely to the lowest of the lowest and the worst of the worst but to all those who might need what was at first called 'preventive' work and, later, 'personal social services'.

7

The development of casework in bureaucratic settings

Beginning in the 1950s and increasingly in the 1960s, importance was attached to 'preventive' work, 'community care' and domiciliary services—all of which were based on what one writer calls 'the conviction that the best place for any individual is his own home' (Forder, 1971). The development of casework in bureaucratic settings occurred in this context. It is a story of the interaction of bureaucratic competition with professionalisation, and the progress of social work educators in influencing the whole ethos of certain social service organisations. Professional social work practice became more closely identified with government social policy.

Investment in preventive services

The case for an increasing governmental investment in preventive services was typically expressed in the following Ministry of Health Circular (1954): 'Local authorities should use their powers to prevent physical and mental ill-health, and so avoid families breaking up, an undesirable state of affairs both because of the bad effects on children and because of the need to provide expensive institutional care.' The 'desirability' part of the argument represented a tendency at this time to idealise the home and the 'united family'. 'Keeping the family together' because a kind of slogan. This emphasis was, perhaps, to some extent a reaction to separation on a large scale occasioned by the war, together with the association of separation with the old Poor Law and, more generally, the legacy of nine-teenth-century social conditions which the welfare state was pledged to erase. The right of families to stay together could, in this sense, be linked with other basic rights, such as the right to work, associated with the welfare state. On the other hand, 'desirability' arguments also reflected fears of the social consequences if family problems were not tackled at an early stage. Force was lent to this argument by the publication in 1951 of John Bowlby's research on the effects of separation from mother in early childhood. As we saw in the last chapter, there was at this time an inclination to see social problems in terms of personal inadequacies and everything from violence and delinquency to illegitimacy, prostitution and low standards could be attributed to 'broken homes'. Later, in the 1960s, the argument began to move from psychological to socio-logical explanations of social problems, including placing more emphasis on the consequences of institutionalisation in prisons, hospitals and homes for the elderly. Develop-ments in medicine and in psychiatry made it possible to discharge patients more quickly from hospitals. For all these reasons, there was an increasing emphasis on keeping patients out of hospitals, children and old people out of care, and offenders out of penal institutions. Correspond-ingly, there was a general increased emphasis on the development of services in the community.

The government circular quoted earlier also indicates an economic argument for keeping the individual in his own home. This was based on the fear that the cost of keeping people in institutions was continually rising, and should be seen in the more general context of apprehen-sion about the costs of other services especially, for ex-ample, the cost of the National Health Service. The cost of keeping children in care, especially in Approved Schools, was an easy and popular target for criticism. Organisations wishing to expand preventive services were able to make use of this situation. Arithmetic calculations were made to justify spending *more* money on appointing casework staff in order to save money on institutional care. FSU did this in order to raise money, especially grants from local authorities whose expenditure might thus be 'saved'.

Local authorities learnt to use the same arguments. Oxfordshire County Council, for example, in 1955 claimed a saving of £15,000 for the cost of one worker. It is not at all clear that this was a valid argument. Packman (1969) suggests a wide range of factors need to be considered in accounting for the rates of admission of children into care in different local authorities, of which the extent of special services provided is only one factor, and in respect of which the evidence is not conclusive.

Settings for the development of casework services

The extension of personal services in the community did not necessarily imply an extension of professional casework. An interesting question is why social work professionalisation occurred in certain settings and not in others. Bearing in mind the very wide field which social work educators had claimed for professional development immediately after the war, and as late as 1950, any one of a wide variety of services could conceivably have provided a setting for the professional development of casework (see chapter 5). For example:

School attendance and education welfare	Youth and Community Work
School Health	Welfare services in industry
Health Visiting	Ministry of Labour
Home help services	Ministry of Pensions
Housing management	National Assistance Board
Youth employment	Various voluntary settings

72

The following areas did, in fact, become settings for the professional development of casework:

Probation
Child Care (fieldwork)
Mental Welfare (fieldwork)
Social Welfare (i.e. the fieldwork
    services of welfare departments)

There was also a modest expansion of medical social work, including some attachments to General Practice (though this did not become widespread), and in the employment of psychiatric social workers in local authorities, mental hospitals and child guidance clinics. Certain voluntary services also developed professionally, for example, moral welfare agencies such as the Edinburgh Guild of Service and certain child care agencies, such as Dr Barnardo's.

Arguments were, in fact, advanced and pressures exercised in favour of many of the areas of work on the first list quoted, as well as for those on the second list. For example, in relation to health visitors, the Jameson Committee Report in 1956 pressed for the recognition of the health visitor as 'the pivotal all-purpose medico-social worker in the home where she should act for all departments of the local authority concerned with health and welfare'. In 1955, a government report on housing stated (Parker, 1965): 'Housing departments must employ skilled staff and these must co-operate closely with other departments, particularly with the welfare departments.' With regard to home helps, the Younghusband Committee Report, in 1959 stated (Parker, 1965): 'Home help organisers should be trained social workers.' In the educational field, a government report on services for maladjusted children published in 1955 said ('Sleeptite Flash', November/December 1955): 'There is no more important aspect of prevention than action designed to keep the family together.' In 1960, the Albemarle Committee stressed the importance of the role of the youth leader in providing preventive services in the community.

There was thus a struggle between various competing bureaucratic interests, each able to advance arguments for developing fieldwork services on professional lines, each based on a particular view or category of explanation of family breakdown. Child care interests, backed by a section of the Home Office, stressed the importance of keeping the family together on economic grounds and to prevent delinquency and child neglect. Health interests, backed by another Ministry, stressed the importance of family services in terms of a broader conception of social and mental health. Whatever the grounds, all the many reports of this period manage to call for increased numbers of workers, usually social workers of one kind or another, and for increased professional training.

There were some opposing voices. The Medical Officer of Health for Kent, for example, in 1957 said ('Sleeptite Flash', September/October 1957):

I have long thought it unfortunate that discussions about the ways of meeting social problems all too frequently resolve themselves into arguments for some new grade of worker. My experience of problem families is that there are already too many social workers, and the addition of one especially trained, whatever that special training may mean, would do very little apart from adding to the cost of the social services.

Barbara Wootton (1959) challenged the whole basis of the definition of, and training for, social work.

The extent to which each interest was successful in obtaining recognition as an appropriate setting for the development of professional casework services, depended on its success in obtaining political and financial backing. A full answer to the question as to why some interests were more successful than others does not seem possible from the limited source material at present available. It is particularly interesting, for example, that education welfare officers failed to achieve the boost in respect of professional social work training which was accorded to social welfare officers. (Education Welfare Officers (or School Attendance Officers) were affected by the professionalisation of both probation and child care services.) One can hazard a guess that social casework interests within the education section of government were weaker than those in the health section.

The consequences of bureaucratic competition in the development of social work were: first, to promote the scale of expansion as a whole; second, to fragment professional social work by engendering vested interests in particular pseudo-subjects based on the application of casework method to so-called specialist settings; and third, to identify social work much more closely with the statutory provision of services and related social policy. Social workers' functions, during this period, were largely determined by Act of parliament.

The 'settings' were administratively, not functionally, determined. Children's departments did *not* deal with the full range of services for children. Welfare services (i.e. in welfare departments) were a rag-bag of services to old people, handicapped people and homeless families. Probation, especially in England and Wales, extended its range of interests into marital work. How could one sensibly talk about 'specialisms' on this basis?

There is one interesting difference in the way social work developed during the first phase of professionalisation up to 1939, in medical and psychiatric social work, and the development of local authority social work in the 1950s and 1960s. In the first phase, on the whole, new posts were created. For example, the first almoners and psychiatric social workers came to newly designated posts —no one had been there before. In the second phase, however, the posts of existing categories of local government officers were taken over and redefined in professional terms. A local government officer, who had originally entered the service 'of local government' with no intention of defining himself as a social worker, went away for 'Younghusband' or child care training and returned one or two years later with a different understanding of what his job was about. When he returned, he had to work alongside his fellow local government officers, some of them waiting to go for training, and a growing number of younger new entrants to social work from the Universities who, perhaps, had yet another perception of their task. This state of confusion of task definition provided a new challenge for social work *as a movement*, namely, to change the ethos of social service departments as a whole. For example, local government officers, who were not professionally trained, were accustomed to keeping a minimum of records, paying their visits to categories of clients at fixed intervals, arriving on time for work, keeping out of their offices most of the day, and communicating within the rigid hierarchy of their departments on a formal basis. Social work as a movement, led by social work educators, tried to change all this. The independently financed National Institute for Social Work Training was in a strong position to play a key role. Social work sections in central government departments also played a part in organising courses which aimed systematically to reach and influence various levels of management. An important part was also played by the Council for Training in Social Work. This was an independent body, whose central function was to approve Certificate in Social Work Courses set up in 1962 by statute, and award the Certificate.

Margot Jeffreys's (1965) study of social welfare in an English county illustrates the difficulties which the distinction between the trained and the untrained groups of workers imposed, and the consequences in terms of the morale of some of the services concerned. Professionalisation forced a fresh definition of the role of certain groups, for example, social welfare officers, while the absence of professionalisation left other groups, such as education welfare officers, uncertain of their existing role.

To add to the confusion, professionalisation took place unevenly. Professionally trained workers tended to congregate in certain areas where professional norms had successfully been established, leaving other areas bereft both of professional influences and of professional staff. While there was a general tendency for professionalism to be further advanced in the south east of England, situations often occurred where neighbouring authorities had reached quite different stages of development. Similarly, within the same authority, different stages were sometimes reached between children's health and welfare departments. Social work as a movement, through the institutions to which we have referred, endeavoured to introduce ideas favourable to professional development in all areas and equally in all departments.

Pressure for a unified local authority department

Another major objective of social workers during this period was the unification of social work as a profession. This was not, at first, easy to attain since, as we have seen, governmental interests promoted further fragmentation of the profession by encouraging separate specialisms to develop in settings associated with particular bureaucratic interests. The Home Office Central Training Council focused on the so-called 'essential ingredients' of child care as a requirement for professional training. The Training Council for Probation made similar demands. Some (but not all) social work educators countered by emphasising the generic content of social casework practice. The struggle was long and occurred in two main areas: first, in promoting legislation to establish unified social work or social service departments and, second, in establishing a unified professional organisation amongst social workers themselves.

In pressing the government for a unified social work department, social workers endeavoured to obtain other professional support. A letter in *The Times*, on 16 March 1955, with a long list of signatories including John Bowlby, Margery Fry, Basil Henriques and Eileen Younghusband, states: 'We are ... convinced that the pressing need of the moment is for the government to appoint a committee of enquiry whose terms of reference should be wide enough to include all classes of family breakdown with positive recommendation for their prevention and alleviation.'

The government, pressed by sectional interests, in fact set up several working parties and committees of enquiry, the principal ones being the Younghusband Working Party (set up in 1955) and, later, the Ingleby Committee (set up in 1956). Each of these committees was limited by its terms of reference which, in turn, reflected the bureaucratic structure which gave rise to the need for the enquiry in the first place. The Younghusband Working Party could not consider the children's services. The Ingleby Committee could not consider the health services. Finally, the Seebohm Committee was appointed which could consider health, welfare and children's services—but not probation. Each report was therefore only able to recommend (among other things, some of which as we shall see later were very important) a unified family service within its own terms of reference. Each stopped short of being able to demand the establishment of a new, single, unified social work department on the lines proposed and accepted in Scotland in the White Paper *Social Work and the Community* published in 1966, which followed the report of the Kilbrandon Committee in 1964.

There were various reasons for the easier passage in Scotland towards unification of social work interests. Bureaucratic interests were different, simpler, and less entrenched. The basis for structural co-ordination already existed within the Scottish Office, which had the effect of filtering away some of the extraneous departmental interests in London. Another reason was that probation in Scotland happened to be a local authority service. Had this been the case in England and Wales it would have been included within the terms of reference of the See-bohm Committee. The principal reason, however, why a unified social work service in Scotland was successfully established was that the proposal sprang from wider and more far-reaching proposals by the Kilbrandon Committee for a new system of juvenile justice. The intention of the Kilbrandon Committee was that the new system of chil-dren's hearings should be backed by a unified local authority service within the framework of an education department. Such a proposal was fully in accordance with the long-standing Scottish tradition of 'social education', some of the origins of which we considered in chapter 2. It was not, however, in accordance with the aims of professional social work in the 1960s. As a result of skilful lobbying independent social work departments thus came into being with the Social Work (Scotland) Act, 1968.

The second area in which the struggle for unification occurred was with professional social work organisations themselves. In 1962, the Association of Social Workers convened a working party which recommended forming a national association based on a minimum qualification in social work. (There was nothing to stop all social workers joining the ASW. Most, however, prior to 1970 when the British Association of Social Workers was formed, preferred to belong to one or another of the 'specialist' bodies.) In 1963, seven organisations combined to form a Standing Conference of Organisations of Social Workers which issued various criteria for professional membership of a body representing 'all social workers'. The British Association of Social Workers did not finally come into being until April 1970.

While social work as a movement aimed to unite professional interests, the professionalising process itself tended to limit the boundaries of professional recognition. Such a limitation was sometimes in conflict with bureaucratic governmental interests in spreading their own boundaries as widely as possible and, in so doing, extending the professionalisation of social work into new areas. The most important example of this was in relation to residential care. Since the residential care of children and child care *fieldwork* services both came within the same section of the Home Office, pressures from this quarter could more easily be exerted to extend professional training and recognition of professional status to residential workers. The Williams Committee, in contrast, taking more detached views, saw the obvious need for training throughout the whole field of residential care, including the care of the elderly. The professional *casework* associations, on the other hand, who claimed to represent professional *social work* as a whole, had to consider warily the grounds on which they could accord the same professional status to residential workers which they accorded to caseworkers. The same sort of question later arose in connection with community workers. This situation was paradoxical. Professional social work organisations, which had pressed the government to extend the scope of social work practice, were now overtaken by events. The various enquiries set up by the government had gone much further than simply calling for a unification of family casework services under a professional umbrella. The social context was changing. The emphasis was moving away from the 'home' to the 'community' and to an emphasis on 'community participation'. The volunteer social worker, as well as the professional, was now receiving greater recognition.

PART III

Social work,
social conflict and bureaucracy

8

The return of the volunteers

A discussion of the role of the voluntary services in the welfare state is complicated by the fact that the word 'voluntary' has a triple meaning. It can mean voluntary as opposed to statutory; voluntary as opposed to professional; or voluntary as opposed to paid. The uses of the term overlap. In accordance with the image of the welfare state it was expected after the war that social services should be systematised and staffed by people who were adequately trained and paid. The image of systematised statutory welfare contrasted with the older images, on the one hand of the discriminating Poor Law, and on the other hand of Lady Bountiful who was usually well meaning but untrained, unpaid and associated with ill-organised non-statutory agencies, or with no organisation at all.

Such imagery, of course, over-simplified the real situation. Many traditional outlets for voluntary (unpaid) social service continued after 1945. These might be through well-established voluntary organisations such as the Red Cross, or through opportunities for unpaid service actually within the statutory system. The latter included the WVS, the London School Care Committees and work associated with the new Maternity and Child Welfare services. It was also recognised that voluntary (non-statutory) agencies could partner statutory services in specific fields of long-

83

standing voluntary concern, for example, in the residential care of children and old people and in services for the blind and deaf.

Voluntary (non-statutory) agencies using voluntary (unpaid) helpers were expected to fulfil perhaps three basic conditions to be acceptable and recognised within the welfare state. First, they were expected to be efficiently organised, to conform to minimum standards and to be co-ordinated with statutory services. Second, they were expected to concentrate on filling gaps in statutory provision and not in duplicating statutory services. Third, if possible they should have a specific contribution to make in the way they provided services. In order to fulfil these conditions after the war, many voluntary organisations grouped together to form national bodies based on an area of interest, such as the National Association for Mental Health (founded in 1946), or locality based organisations such as local Councils of Social Service. Many existing agencies redefined their terms of reference to suit the new post-war situation dominated by the idea that basic physical needs would be met by the state. The Annual Report for Dr Barnardo's for 1946, for example (quoted by Beveridge, 1948), states: 'Destitution as known in the Victorian era has been replaced by what one might term moral destitution.' Beveridge himself, in his book *Voluntary Action*, stressed the continuing role for voluntary agencies and called for government action to support voluntary effort in certain specific respects, including the promotion of mutual aid societies in the field of social security.

In talking about 'the return of the volunteers' later on, therefore, in the late 1950s and in the 1960s, one should understand that they never completely left the scene of social service after the war. Indeed, whatever might in theory be their more restricted role in the age of statutory provision, there were some prepared to argue that the welfare state made voluntary activity more, and not less, important—in the same way that some were prepared to argue the importance of professional casework in the age of the wholesale provision of basic services. There were three areas of expanding voluntary activity after the war which were, indeed, especially important.

Family-focused services

First, there was increased voluntary interest in family-focused services. Apart from Family Service Units, which we discussed in chapter 6, there were other services associated with the idealisation of the united family and with the goal of keeping the family together. It has been suggested, for example, that the Marriage Guidance Councils were significant in this respect. Founded in 1938, it was only after the war that they developed their personal counselling services on a voluntary (unpaid) basis. Morris (1969) suggests:

> The fact that the number of broken marriages increased greatly during and after the war was doubtless responsible for the urgency with which the M.G.C. set about its task. The movement had the support of people like probation officers, doctors, parsons, teachers and social workers, whose work brought them up against marital problems.

The idealisation of the community

Second, there was an increased interest in voluntary activity associated with the idealisation of the local community and, in particular, with the movement which promoted the building of village halls, and community centres. Legislation in 1936 first enabled local housing authorities to provide community centres. The Education Act of 1944 obliged local authorities to secure facilities for 'leisure time occupations' and at the same time empowered education authorities to provide 'places' where

85

such facilities could be employed (Kuenstler, 1961). The activities of Rural Community Councils and other voluntary bodies ensured that this provision was not as ineffective as the provision for health centres in the National Health Service Act proved to be. By exercising continual pressures and by raising money voluntarily 800 community centres were built between 1945 and 1960. This process by which the government encouraged voluntary organisations to play a part in pressing for better facilities from government resources later became common in other fields.

Services for the elderly

The third particularly important area of voluntary activity after the war was in relation to the needs of the elderly. A National Old People's Welfare Committee founded in 1940 was reconstituted as a Council to co-ordinate an increasing volume of voluntary activity after the war, and to draw attention to the needs of the elderly by educational means, and to press for better provisions. Its activities included political lobbying. The absence of an 'old persons act' to correspond with the new Children's Act 1948 was an obvious structural deficiency in the post-war system of social services. The government's unwillingness to do anything more than call for greater co-ordination of services in the early 1950s was typical of the unwillingness of government to admit deficiencies in the system, which we have discussed earlier in chapter 6, and which was paralleled in the area of family services. The significance of the popular movement sponsored by the National Old People's Welfare Council for a more comprehensive social service for the elderly was that it revealed the absence of adequate services was not just an unfortunate oversight in planning, or a gap to be filled by a voluntary organisation, but symptomatic of basic inadequacies in the system. Pensions were too low. Housing was inadequate. Residential care was unimaginative. Health provisions were unco-ordinated or neglected. Welfare provisions in the home were unevenly available. From the end of the 1950s the number of social surveys on the needs of the elderly which revealed these inadequacies greatly increased. But they also led on to other surveys of a more general kind. The 'discovery' of the problem of the elderly in the 1950s led directly to the 'discovery' of the problem of poverty in the 1960s.

The peace movement and voluntary social service

Towards the end of the 1950s the scope of voluntary activity widened, and its context began to change. Voluntary (unpaid) service came to be less associated with the middle aged, and more with the young; less with the middle classes and more with a wider social spectrum including (according to a contemporary writer) 'industrial apprentices, police cadets, clerks, secretaries, and factory workers' (quoted from Morris, 1969); less with respectability and more with social protest. The social process and the sequence of events involved in these changes are complex. It is perhaps convenient to begin with a discussion of the relevance of the peace movement in Britain in the period from about 1958 to 1963.

As several writers have pointed out, there was a connection between social work, social protest and the peace movement in Britain. Bessel (1970) narrows the link to the association of Jane Addams in the American settlement movement, and adds: 'Among other things, she led a peace mission right through Europe during the first world war, and it is from her work that many of the peace movements of the present day are derived.' In our view the links are broader and more basic. The link between 'peace', 'harmony', 'charity' and 'social work' was implicit in the origins of social work as a movement, and in at least one of the three traditions—namely direct social action—

87

on which it was founded (see chapter 2).

The Bomb in the late 1950s perhaps symbolised the distance the state could travel away from the idealised concept of welfare. Much of the propaganda of the Campaign for Nuclear Disarmament consisted of comparisons between amounts spent on the Bomb and on the social services. The peace movement gave to many the confidence to challenge the authority and the credibility of the state. But *political* protest was frustrating and unrewarding. After the first few years of confidence when singing songs and marching appeared to be making inroads into the centres of power—at least in relation to the Labour Party, the trade union movement and the churches—there followed a period of disillusionment with the political processes. While mass civil disobedience met with no more success than constitutional protest, it did lead many people on to ask more searching questions about the nature of a society which could both manufacture the Bomb and frustrate the efforts of those who wanted to achieve even limited political objectives. While some supporters in the early 1960s moved away from activity altogether, others moved to a broader basis for challenging the political and social system as a whole. Disillusionment with a centralised, atrophied system of government suggested the alternative of local community politics, community based action, and a focus on local issues such as a lack of playgrounds and an identification with the unfortunates in society who were victimised by, and were powerless to change, the 'system'. The Committee of One Hundred, in its later years of existence, turned its attention from bombs to boy soldiers, gypsies, squatters and homeless families. New radical community based organisations sprang up associated in their origin closely with the peace movement, such as the Simon Community. The Simon Community was not only a means of assisting alcoholics and other social misfits in the welfare state: it was seen by its members as demonstrating a process of personal involvement and identification with human need. In so doing, it was suggestive of the possibility of an alternative society.

The idea of an alternative society was also suggested through the activities of another section of the peace movement, namely work camps. Here the emphasis had, from the start before the war, been on alternative constructive action, originally an alternative to military service. After the war, the work camp movement linked peace with international understanding and social service. The International Voluntary Service for Peace, dropped the 'peace' from its title to gain wider support (in much the same way that Pacifist Service Units changed its name to Family Service Units) and placed more emphasis on local groups engaging in local community service. From the late 1950s the movement grew rapidly. It attracted young people searching for constructive gestures with social meaning.

Meanwhile developments in thinking about the social services themselves were indicating potential areas for increased voluntary (community based) interest.

First, the idea of 'keeping the family together' which characterised the post-war period was extended to 'keeping the community together', in Michael Young and Peter Willmott's book *Family and Kinship in East London* (1957). This study was also important in revealing the need for research and consultation in planning—consultation with those who would be affected, namely the local community. Volunteers saw in the issues raised in this and other studies of communities the opportunity and the need for community organisation or community action to demand attention from authority.

Second, new thinking about the adverse affects of institutionalisation coincided with developments in medicine and psychiatry which rendered the need for residential treatment less prolonged. This, in turn, focused attention on the need for better community services and for more

89

education of the public. Hospitals, prisons and old people's homes could not just simply be emptied. The community had to be educated into accepting the inmates in their midst. Thus an awareness of the dehumanising effects of institutions was coupled with a growing movement to humanise the community. This particular movement also brought together the two main wings of voluntary service in the 1960s, the traditional and the radical, the old and the new. They often had separate organisations: for example, the Discharged Prisoners' Aid Society (dating from the nineteenth century) was old and respectable; Norman House, started by Merfyn Turner, was young and innovatory. The ideology was different, but the concrete goals were shared. There was a desperate need for half-way houses.

Third, there was a growing emphasis at this time on the value of consumer based, mutual aid and self-help groups in the community as opposed to services rendered within a more traditional, paternalistic framework. The 1960s saw the spectacular growth of various groups of disabled people, for example. The popular mood for consumer based services was typified by the growth of the Consumers' Association itself, initiated by Michael Young of the Institute for Community Studies. The concept spread from 'Which?' brand of soap powder, to 'Where?' to send your child to school, and to groups of the consumers of the social services, such as hospital patients' associations and, more recently, to the Claimants' Union of those in receipt of supplementary benefits.

Race relations

While the emptying of long-stay institutions provided one major challenge to the humanity and social concern of the community, another major challenge came from an awareness of the question of race relations. In 1950 there were 100,000 coloured people in Britain. By 1968 there were ten times as many, including families who came to join their men-folk. The accepted social principles of 'keeping the family together' and of 'keeping the community together' were both in conflict with racial prejudice and fear of competition for scarce resources in housing and, in some areas, employment. This situation presented a challenge to various traditions in voluntary social action. It could be seen, for example, as an opportunity to practise conflict resolution, as an opportunity for radical community action for better services, or as an opportunity to demonstrate co-operation between statutory and voluntary effort.

Revival of direct social action

Whether the pursuit of personal social service derived from disillusionment with power politics, or from other motives, some of the movements associated with voluntary effort in the 1960s bear a striking similarity to the tradition of direct social action in the nineteenth century which we discussed in chapter 2. Both could be described as the expression of a militant social pacifism which, indeed, is an important thread that runs continuously through the history of social work as a movement in Britain. The idea of an alternative society, the obsession with the notion of community, the implicit belief in social education as a means of effecting change and the ambiguity with regard to what was meant by 'political', underlay the dynamic initiative of, say, Merfyn Turner, as it had the work of, say, Canon Barnett. One movement, in fact, in the 1960s, Factories for Peace was consciously modelled on a revival of Owenism (trading under the name 'Rowen'). For the most part, however, the 'direct social action' of the 1960s was less romantic, less dependent on personalities, more democratic and more limited in scope than the efforts of the radical social pacifists of the nineteenth century. Typical, for example, was the National

Association of Pre-School Play Groups, founded in 1961 'as the direct result of one mother's letter to the press welcoming enquiries from mothers and teachers who would like to create their own solutions to these problems' (Morris, 1969). In its own publication it stated: 'Some mothers are not prepared to wait for the government and action by a handful of enthusiasts has resulted in a nationwide movement.' By 1968, some 3,000 children were being catered for (Morris, 1969).

The attitude of the government, in the meantime, was to say repeatedly that it welcomed voluntary action of this kind, although it was less forthcoming in meeting the demands direct action groups actually made. In particular, both the Disablement Income Group and the Child Poverty Action Group were only partially successful in winning from governments the measures they considered necessary.

During the 1960s successive government reports and circulars expressed an enthusiasm for voluntary effort, for example, in the health and welfare fields, in education, in mental health, in probation and aftercare and in community relations. In these reports and statements, the grounds for support can be seen to change from the argument about filling gaps in social service provision (which, as we have seen, was the general argument for voluntary social services in the 1950s) to arguments based on a theory of community development; that is to say the argument that community and consumer participation would help to identify areas of need and lead to the more effective allocation of resources. This was the pattern already established in the movement for community centres. Thus, for example, an official statement on the development of community care in the health and welfare services, issued in 1963, states (Morris, 1969):

The aim of enabling the mentally disordered to take their part in the life of the community cannot be realised without the co-operation of the public ... In no other aspect of health and welfare is it so necessary to demonstrate the existence of the need in order to be able to meet it. The participation of voluntary organisations in all kinds of work for the mentally disordered is all the more valuable for this reason.

The same sort of argument was later used in relation to the work of the Community Relations Commission and in support of the idea of Community Development Projects. It did not necessarily follow, however, that all the voluntary organisations concerned accepted this theory which assumed that there still existed a basic consensus of interest between the state and the citizen within the community. We shall be considering this problem in chapter 9.

The attitude of governments also assumed that there was a basic community of interest between the voluntary (untrained) worker and the professional social worker in the welfare state. This was not always the case, as the evidence presented to the Aves (1969) Committee showed. Sometimes volunteers were seen by professional social workers as rivals to clients for their attention and sometimes volunteers saw themselves as competitors with professionals. The evidence, however, suggests that 'professional' was often equated with 'official' in the eyes of the volunteers (and in the eyes of clients) and this does less than justice to the movement within professional social work, which we discussed in the last chapter, to alter the official-bound milieu of the statutory social service agency, in favour of a greater flexibility and orientation to the needs of the client.

There was one voluntary organisation in the 1960s which was particularly interesting as an alternative to professional casework. The Samaritans offered an alternative service to those who, in a crisis, wanted someone anonymously to listen to their account of personal problems and distress. What the Samaritans lacked in professional social work education they gained in being able to offer immediate attention, the assurance of confidentiality, personal sympathy and skill in listening, and all in a setting uncluttered by bureaucracy, yet with access to professional resources where necessary. Surely their success should have challenged professional social workers more than it did?

There may be two reasons why it did not challenge professional social workers. First, the Samaritans were largely chosen from the middle classes and they do not seem to have been very concerned to press their claims in relation to the claims of professional social workers whom they regarded sometimes as consultants. Second, professional social workers, on their part, were preoccupied with building up their own professional organisation and unified approach to training and pressing for a single local authority setting in which to practise. The latent challenge of the Samaritans was not pressed on either side. Indeed the whole question of the relationship between the professional and the voluntary social worker was largely evaded at this time.

9

Implications of the retreat from the welfare state

In Part II we suggested that both advocates and critics of the welfare state had accepted basic myths instead of facing the reality that what had been conceived as an 'ideal' system was, in fact, a compromise between political, bureaucratic and professional interests. We also saw that towards the end of the 1950s the myth began to be exploded.

The point we shall now consider in this present chapter is that at the same time that the myth was exposed, the government's political commitment to the ideal was visibly relaxed. The effect of this was to broaden the scope of social work.

Controversy over the relaxation of the political commitment to welfare occurred symbolically over prescription charges, in 1952. While some people saw the decision to impose 1s. charge merely as an expedient to check alleged abuse of free drugs, and to assuage apprehension about the rising costs of the health service, others saw it as a fundamental inroad into the ideology of the National Health service, namely that it should be freely available to all citizens.

Not everybody had to pay the new prescription charges. Children were exempt. Those in receipt of national assistance could reclaim the charges imposed. These concessions were not in themselves contentious, but what some found disturbing was the implied distinction between certain classes in the community. The imposition of prescription charges could be seen, at worst, to presage a return to the pre-war situation where the dreaded means test exposed the differences between the 'haves' and the 'have-nots' in society. It was correctly predicted that the measure was a precedent. Other charges were introduced within the National Health service and elsewhere. Rent controls, for example, were relaxed in 1957. Council house rents rose to be closer to a so-called economic rent, and local authorities were empowered to introduce rent-rebate schemes for those who could not afford the higher rents. This, again, increased an awareness of the distinction between the 'poor' and the rest of the population. A similar pattern of service developed in education welfare.

But was it the poor who were really benefiting? It was at least arguable that tax allowances favoured the middle classes at the expense of the working class. Moreover, apart from the chipping away at the fabric of social welfare, the government's social and economic policies seemed increasingly to undermine a commitment to the welfare of the working classes. From the early 1960s unemployment slowly began to rise from the very low levels of the 1950s. Price rises hit hardest at basic essentials. The image of the affluent society increasingly raised the question, 'affluent for whom?'

Yet the expectation that the state was the appropriate institution to promote the welfare of all its citizens, but particularly the poorest, remained. Few people argued, for example, that industry should accept a positive social responsibility to provide welfare services or conduct business on the basis of recognising social as well as economic costs (except with government inducements to do this). Even nationalised industries were expected to be run on a commercial profit-making basis, including the railways. Again, while the government encouraged voluntary social service provision, no one seriously suggested a return to large-scale private philanthropy as the means to cope with social distress. The government still had the responsibility for welfare, if on a diminished and more selective basis. Social work, with its tradition of individualising social problems, and now much more identified with the state than in the past, became the ideal institution to promote social welfare.

The extended scope of social work

The scope of professional social work was extended in three specific respects. First, social workers had a specific responsibility to ensure that clients were claiming all the benefits to which they were entitled and that they were aware of all the exemptions from welfare charges which might apply to their situation. This meant that social workers had to be much more concerned with simply giving information. As previously, they had to go on from here to look at individual situations where there might be underlying non-material needs. Second, social workers had a responsibility to ensure an equitable distribution of material resources over which their agencies had direct control. Such resources were increasing. The Children and Young Persons Act, 1963, gave to children's departments (later social service departments) the power to disburse material help under certain circumstances. Third, social workers were increasingly given duties to assist groups and communities as well as individuals.

Pressure to broaden the scope of social work came at the same time that social workers were themselves pressing for a unified service within which to practise. Originally the demand had been for a unified setting in which to practise family casework, child care, mental welfare, and other forms of specialist help, but the question of unification developed into a question of the kinds of material resources required to be at hand for social work

97

practice. Thus the Seebohm Committee (paragraph 131) considered, but rejected, a proposal for a unified department based *merely* on the amalgamation of social case-work services and called, instead, for a department which would include other resources: 'The proposed social case-work department would not have enough control of residential and other services to enable it to do its work. Relationships between departments would be uncertain because social work does not consist only of casework.' A new concept came into existence towards the end of the 1960s, namely 'social work services', or those services and resources directly necessary or ancillary to the exercise of professional social work practice. The inclusion or exclusion of particular resources in this new concept was arbitrary, and determined by administrative traditions and bureaucratic wrangling as much as by rational argument. Whether home helps or health visitors were 'in' or 'out' was perhaps a bureaucratic question rather than a question answered in accordance with any systematic study of client needs. But however large or small the new category of resources, the idea of social work services was itself important in recognising that social work was no longer concerned merely with the provision of 'the casework relationship' to enable individuals and families to benefit from the welfare services of a society committed to the welfare of the whole community, but that instead social work itself had to be concerned with the adequacy of provisions, with disbursing resources and with groups and communities as well as with individuals. Social work also, it was claimed, had to be concerned with social research and with the assessment of social needs upon which social policies should be based.

The extended scope of social work placed its organisations in a bureaucratic dilemma. Social work was now more clearly identified with authority and the resources of social work services had to be organised. This implied the development of bureaucratic structures. On the other

hand, after the Seebohm Committee Report, and other official reports and circulars, there were calls for greater community participation and an orientation to the principle of
self-determination. Having seen themselves as a humanising agent in relation to the administrative structures of
the welfare state, social workers now had to face the challenge of being an organisation within state bureaucracy
themselves and at the same time expected to be identified
with the local community they served.

Social workers also faced a professional dilemma. If it
could no longer be assumed that the state had a total commitment to welfare and to universal provision, and if,
indeed, there was (as some claimed) a bias towards the
interests of the middle classes, what should social workers
do? If they remained politically passive, they could be
seen as agents of a political establishment which did not
share the values on which social work as a movement
was based. If they became politically active, on the other
hand, questions arose about loyalties to their employing
organisations. Moreover, it was part of the professional
ethic to keep politics out of casework, if not community
work (and social workers still saw themselves primarily
as caseworkers). What did professionalism mean in this
respect? Did it mean a guarantee to one's employer of
neutrality when political considerations entered decision-
making? Or did it mean the right to take up a political
position independent of the position of one's employer?

While professional social workers had to struggle with
these dilemmas, voluntary (non-statutory or unpaid) social
workers were politically less inhibited. We have noted previously that during the 1960s there tended to be a split
between professional social work interests and some of the
voluntary organisations engaged in radical activity. Professional social workers, on the whole, were politically
active only in matters which promoted social work interests
as a profession, or which aimed to influence social service
organisations in placing more emphasis on the needs of

individual clients. The gap, indeed, between professional social work and radical organisations was so great that some groups used the term 'anti-social work'. These groups whose activities were thoroughly in keeping with the traditions of the social work movement felt, nevertheless, unable to identify with contemporary social work. For them, the term professional was synonymous with bureaucratic.

Inadequate service provision

Thus it was the voluntary (non-professional) organisations, rather than the professional bodies, which exposed areas of inadequate service provision, which lobbied the government or engaged in direct social action. For example, it was the Child Poverty Action Group, not the Association of Child Care Officers, which played the major role in the re-discovery of poverty in the mid-1960s (although ACCO claimed a better record of social action than the other professional bodies). It was a voluntary body, the Disablement Income Group, not the Institute of Social Welfare, which led the way in exposing the needs of handicapped people and in pressing for legislation. It was the National Association of Mental Health, not the Association of Psychiatric Social Workers or the Society of Mental Welfare Officers, which pioneered the mental health movement. In the field of housing, it was a voluntary organisation, Shelter, not the Association of Family Caseworkers, which publicised the nature and extent of un-met housing needs. In relation to the homeless, gypsies, the social isolate, and other 'misfits', it was small direct action groups which drew the public's attention to injustices, not the Association of Social Workers. To be fair, of course, individual professional workers played a part in voluntary action outside their professional organisations. But their numbers were small.

On the positive side, professional social work did succeed

in breaking free of the restrictions of specific settings. Case-work practice became less related to minimum statutory duties and more 'family' orientated. Even so-called family casework in the 1950s had often been interpreted narrowly as working with mothers in relation to children. In the 1960s, more conscious attempts were made to bring fathers into the picture and to consider the extended family.

Moreover, in spite of the tendency of professional social work to become bureaucratised in the eyes of more radical volunteers (and perhaps in the eyes of clients), increasing numbers of people in the 1960s were attracted to courses of professional training. New recruits to professional social work often brought with them pre-course experience from the voluntary field. Slowly, social work education accepted the need to aim to radicalise professional social work prac-tice in accordance with a changing social context where social injustice was more visible. The professional litera-ture, particularly the journals, gave increasing emphasis to the place of radical social action within professional social work practice.

10

The bureaucratic interest
in community work

Community work, in the sense of social work with communities, has a long tradition in Britain. It was an integral part of social work founded as a movement at the end of the nineteenth century. (It is difficult to think of any technique of modern community work which was not experimented with between 1895 and 1910.) What occurred thereafter was not (as is often suggested) the demise of community work in Britain and its development in the United States, but a different kind of development in Britain, associated with different institutions. This was the consequence of the interaction between the professional 'movement' and bureaucratic influences during the first phase of the development of social work, which we discussed in chapter 4. As casework developed professionally, it leaned increasingly towards psychiatry for its conceptual framework, using terms like 'diagnosis', and 'transference'. Casework was practised chiefly in settings which, broadly speaking, related to health services: mental and general hospitals, and local authority health departments. With the exception of child guidance, it had little to do with administrative settings related to the field of education. As community work became professionalised, on the other hand, it leaned towards educational concepts like 'programme' and 'activities' and it developed in settings closely related to educational rather than health interests. Thus, for a long time and especially between the two world wars community work in Britain was closely associated with adult education, youth work and the use of community centres.

The objectives of community work (even more than casework) have varied in accordance with the social and political context. At the time of the arrival of the welfare state, for example, community work in Britain either meant promoting a sense of community fellowship or it meant the co-ordination of statutory and voluntary services to help the whole community. This did not mean that it was politically inactive, as the movement for community centres or the concern for the elderly, bears witness. From the late 1950s the movement to take people out of institutions and to treat them in their own homes altered the context from 'fellowship' to 'community care', and this also extended health and social work interests more directly into the field of community work. In the 1960s, the exposure of the inadequacies of welfare provisions, the growing confidence in private individuals taking direct action to achieve social objectives, the relaxation of the political commitment to welfare by government, and the general process of democratisation with emphasis on the idea of 'community participation', opened the doors to a wider range of involvement in community work. The current bureaucratic interest in community work—including not only that of social work organisations, but education, planning, health, race relations and other 'angles'—arises in this context.

The organisational context

This aspect of the development of community work is complicated not just because community work has become almost anybody's business but because each change in the social context has produced new types of institutions.

These institutions remained after the context changed and in varying degrees managed to adapt to new circumstances. Settlements, for example, have shown a high degree of adaptability to changed demands at different times. The same is true of Councils of Social Service. Yet there is no uniformity of approach amongst individual Settlements, or individual Councils of Social Service, so that one cannot talk about the 'Settlement approach' to community work. Each Settlement has adapted differently.

Apart from voluntary (non-statutory) organisations, a wide range of other bodies, including commercial organisations, have in the past had a general interest in aspects of community work. Such organisations include denominational as well as inter-denominational church groups, self-help groups, mutual benefit societies, trade unions, co-operative societies and, in some cases, private industry. Some of the most comprehensive schemes for social planning, since New Lanark, were pioneered at Bournville, New Earswick and elsewhere through the provision of capital from private industry. Today, when community work conveys panacean images of 'self-help in the community', any of these institutions could conceivably seek to revive an historic interest—and some of them are doing so (for example, the Workers' Educational Association).

The pattern of the statutory organisations' interest in community work in some ways resembles the bureaucratic competition for the provision of professional casework services, which we discussed in chapter 7, with recurrent calls for professional training, increased establishments, and co-ordination of effort.

The first major claim to community work was, as we have said earlier, made by education interests—both at central and local government levels. The 1944 Education Act consolidated and extended earlier legislation enabling local education authorities to develop youth and community services including the provision of recreational centres. The general claim that education was linked with a need to expand into community work has been made from various starting points. First, education does not end with schooling and further education must include a concern *for* the community, and be rooted in a response *from* the community. Second a school, especially a comprehensive school, may provide a natural focus for developing the life of a community, through parent–teacher associations or other means. Third, schools have recently been moving into the field of school counselling services. (The word 'counselling', used in Britain in educational and psychological circles, as well as by the Samaritans and the Marriage Guidance Council, is an interesting alternative to the word 'casework'. The former is often a means of establishing a demarcation from professional social work.) Fourth, there is a movement to extend community interest in relation to the provision of nursery schools. Fifth, education is concerned with the problem of cultural poverty and, therefore, with so-called culturally deprived areas. This led to the designation of experimental projects associated with 'educational priority areas' following the Plowden Committee Report. Finally, there is the youth service itself, with more emphasis on 'community service' following the Albemarle Committee Report (Ministry of Education, 1960).

A second area in which there is a traditional statutory claim to community work is housing. Housing authorities have powers to make accommodation available as advice centres to other statutory or voluntary interests, and some authorities have shown an interest in neighbourhood advice centres. The first legislation in relation to community work in Britain was, perhaps, the Housing Act of 1936 which enabled local authorities to provide community centres. Housing Departments in large cities, such as Birmingham, have appointed community development teams to help to plan re-housing programmes.

Third, and more recently, sections of the Home Office have promoted developments in community work. These

include community development projects in areas designated as having high need. In addition community relations projects have been sponsored by the Community
Relations Commission, set up under the Race Relations
Act, 1968, 'to encourage the establishment of harmonious
community relations' and to advise the Home Secretary
on matters relating to racial integration. If there is a
common thread running through these projects it is perhaps the aim of forestalling community dissatisfaction and
thereby understanding in advance a potential threat to
law and order. The police, too, have been involved in
community projects and the Home Office is anxious to
show a positive concern for community relations as a
foundation for effective social control.

Fourth, the Department of the Environment, and local
planning authorities and Clerks' Departments, sometimes
have an interest in community work. Here again, there are
several possible points of departure. The emphasis may
be on social planning to accompany physical planning
based, where possible, on community participation, in
decisions affecting the formulation and implementation of
plans. The Skeffington Committee Report of 1969 suggested the appointment of yet another kind of community
development officer for this purpose. Some New Towns
have 'Social Development Officers'. Community work may
also be an aspect of regional planning and it may also be
involved in the notion, at the other extreme, of neighbourhood councils, within a reformed system of local government. In many of these respects, government agencies are
building on the experience of voluntary agencies, and
reviving earlier traditions associated with voluntary planning or schemes for community participation.

Fifth, health interests have extended into the field of
community work, often associated with the idea of community care. Yet again, there are several starting-points. It
can be applied, for example, in relation to the building of
health centres. It is more usually applied specifically in

the mental health field, around the ideology of social psychiatry, or of preventive psychiatry. In this respect, hospitals have extended their services into the community, seeing the hospital increasingly as a community health centre rather than as a place of residence.

Finally, social work (Scotland), and social service (England and Wales) departments have themselves ventured directly into the field of community work. Specifically, for example, social work or social service departments inherited from children's departments the idea of providing advice centres under the Children and Young Persons Act 1963, the encouragement to promote community care facilities under the Mental Health Acts 1959 (England and Wales) and 1960 (Scotland), while encouragement to promote community facilities for the disabled has since been extended by the Chronically Sick and Disabled Persons Act 1970. Apart from having a direct responsibility for certain aspects of community work, local authority social work or social service departments have a general remit to co-ordinate and promote community services as a whole, and various reports and circulars lay particular stress on this duty. The following extract from a Scottish Circular (swsg, 1968) states this as follows:

To promote social welfare covers all the categories of people who are eligible for services of advice, support or care from a local authority under any legislation. It covers also those people who do not come within any identifiable category except that they are in need of some form of advice, guidance or assistance in dealing with a personal difficulty ... The duty to promote social welfare must include concern for groups of people, whether families or other small groups or larger groups forming, for example, the population of a particular part of a local authority's area. Moreover the duty is not only that of reacting to known needs ... the local authority should seek out existing needs which have not yet been brought to the authority's attention, identify

incipient needs, and try to influence social and environ-
mental developments in such ways as will not only
prevent the creation of social difficulties but will posi-
tively lead to the creation of good social conditions.

Comparison with bureaucratic interest in casework

At the present time we are too close to events, and there
is not enough material available, to discern what is happen-
ing in relation to the bureaucratic interest in community
work, but we can make one or two tentative observations
in comparing it with the earlier bureaucratic claims to
preventive casework in the late 1950s and early 1960s
(which we discussed in chapter 7). It *may* be that the
current interest in community work is less dominated by
the bureaucratic claims to the merits of one particular
setting as compared with other settings. Theorists are *not*
busy producing textbooks about, say, 'community development in housing' or 'community development in planning'
in the way in which theorists produced texts about 'casework in child care' in the early 1960s. There is not the
same urge to define, say, 'the essential ingredients of community work in community relations' as there was previously to define 'the essential ingredients in child care' or
in probation. Instead, broader questions are being asked
about the ideological orientation of community work, and
theoretical attempts are being made to distinguish different levels of work, irrespective of the sponsorship. Community work may be practised at a neighbourhood level,
or at levels removed from direct contact with individual
'citizens' as 'citizens'. On the other hand, there is much
confusion about terminology (Leaper, 1971), and in the
training for community work, which render the recognition of community work courses and qualifications a
jungle as meaningless as the educational jungle of casework training of a few years ago. In the present struggle
between competing interests, colleges of education, extra-

mural departments and other teaching interests may argue with considerable historical justification that community work has more to do with teaching and with youth work than with professional social work.

The question of training for community work raises again the wider question of how far social work can be considered as a profession and how far it can be considered as a social movement. The community worker *cannot* define his objectives and methods simply in professional 'personal service' terms. He is concerned with social ideals, aspirations of people and with institutions as well as sometimes with 'problems' requiring professional attention. He *must* be involved with volunteers.

We have suggested in this book that the historical meaning of social work can only be understood in terms wider than those contained within the history of relatively small groups of professionally trained social workers (who are still mainly caseworkers). The attempt to define social work solely in professional terms invites the comment (Wilensky and Lebaux, 1965): 'No group can claim a monopoly of humanitarian philosophy or create a profession out of it.' Social work as one application of a humanitarian philosophy can be more usefully considered as a social movement, the historical roots of which we have traced, and the need for which today is widely recognised. In this way we can make useful connections between the various activities which constitute social work, including community work, and between the tasks of the professionally trained, the untrained and the volunteer social worker. Only in this way will the professional contribution to social work in the long run prove more credible than the philanthropy it replaced.

Further reading

There are very few recent books specifically about the history of social work in Britain. Young and Ashton (1956) can be regarded as a source of reference so far as the nineteenth century is concerned. Woodroofe (1966) links the nineteenth with the twentieth century, and developments in Britain and the United States. It is useful to read a general social history in conjunction with a book specifically about the history of social work, and I would suggest Gregg (1970). For those who like original documents, Rose (1971) contains a useful collection, including some material relating to the Charity Organisation Society. McLaughlin (1969) is useful background reading on social movements and Pinker (1971) on social theory and social policy. Many of the other books I would like to recommend are unfortunately out of print, and some may be difficult to find, but I have included some of these in the following selection of one or two books for each chapter:

Chapter 1
Owen (1965) A general account of the development of philanthropy.

Chapter 2
Beveridge (1948) This includes brief accounts of prominent people engaged in social action in the nineteenth century.

Kirkman-Gray (1908) Well worth reading, if it can be found.

Chapter 3
Reason (1898) Accounts of work associated with the Settlement movement. Very useful, and probably hard to find.

Smith (1965) A little book with a chapter on the origins of social work education, but not as useful as contemporary sources.

Chapter 4
Richmond (1915) Although written in America, this throws light on the way in which social work came to be conceptualised in professional terms. For a long time it was regarded as a classic text-book both in Britain and America. (Well worth reading today, from that point of view too.) Has had many reprints.

Chapter 5
Schottland (1967) A collection of short articles by many authors, on the welfare state.

Chapter 6
Hall (1952) The chapter on problem families in the first edition.

Chapter 7
Parker (1965) Particularly deals with the relations between central and local government and the demand for preventive health and welfare services (including children's services).

Jeffreys (1965) Describes the consequences, in one area, namely Buckinghamshire.

Chapter 8
Morris (1969) A useful survey of the voluntary scene.

Chapter 9
Titmuss (1958)   A classic, and still worth reading.

Chapter 10
Kuenstler (1961)   A useful symposium on the development of ideas about community work in Britain up to
   1960.
Leaper (1971)   Gives a recent account.

Bibliography

ALBEMARLE REPORT *see* MINISTRY OF EDUCATION (1960).

ANGUS, M. (1913) 'Sheriff Watson of Aberdeen', *Aberdeen Daily Journal*.

AVES, G. (1969) 'Report of a Committee jointly set up by the National Council of Social Service and the National Institute for Social Work Training', *The Volunteer Worker in the Social Services*, Allen & Unwin.

BARNETT, CANON and MRS E. (1915) *Practical Socialism*, Longmans.

BARNETT, S. (1896) *What is Toynbee Hall?* Toynbee Hall, London.

BARTLETT, H. M. (1940, reprinted 1964) *Some Aspects of Social Casework in a Medical Setting*, National Association of Social Workers, New York.

BELL, E. H. C. M. (1942) *Octavia Hill: A Biography*, Constable.

BESSEL, R. (1970) *Introduction to Social Work*, Batsford.

BEVERIDGE, W. (1942) *Social Insurance and the Allied Services*, HMSO.

BEVERIDGE, W. (1948) *Voluntary Action*, Macmillan.

BIESTEK, F. P. (1957) *The Casework Relationship*, Allen & Unwin.

BOULDING, K. (1958) *The Image*, University of Michigan Press.

BOWLBY, J. (1951) *Maternal Care and Mental Health*, World Health Organisation.

BOWLE, J. (1954) *Politics and Opinion in the Nineteenth Century*, Cape.

CARLEBACH, J. (1970) *Caring for Children in Trouble*, Routledge & Kegan Paul.

CARPENTER, J. E. (1879) *The Life and Work of Mary Carpenter*, London.

CARTER, A. (1970) *Direct Action*, Housmans.

CAVENAGH, W. E. (undated) *Four Decades of Students in Social Work*, Research Board, Faculty of Commerce and Social Studies, University of Birmingham (monograph, limited edition).

113

BIBLIOGRAPHY

CHARITY ORGANISATION SOCIETY *Annual Report*, 1899, 1900.
COLE, G. D. H. (1947) *The Intelligent Man's Guide to the Post-War World*, Gollancz.
CORDER, S. (1853) *Life of Elizabeth Fry*, London.
DONNISON, D. V. (1967) *The Government of Housing*, Pelican.
FORDER, A. (ed.) (1971) *Penelope Hall's Social Services of England and Wales*, Routledge & Kegan Paul.
FOUCAULT, M. (1967) *Madness and Civilisation*, Tavistock.
FRY, A. R. (1935) *John Bellers, Quaker Economist and Social Reformer*, Cassell.
GERANDO, BARON DE (1833) *The Visitor of the Poor*, London.
GORE, M. S. (1957) *Social Work in India*, Asia Publishing House.
GREGG, P. (1970) *A Social and Economic History of Britain, 1760-1960*, Harrap.
HALL, P. M. P. (1952) *The Social Services of Modern England*, Routledge & Kegan Paul.
HALMOS, P. (1965) *The Faith of the Counsellors*, Constable.
HAMILTON, G. (1940, reprinted 1964) *Theory and Practice of Social Casework*, Columbia University Press.
HARRISON, B. (1966) 'Philanthropy and the Victorians', *Victorian Studies*, Vol. IX, June, Indiana University Press.
HOBSBAWM, E. J. (ed.) (1969) *Frederick Engels: The Condition of the Working Class in England*, Panther.
HOME OFFICE (1960) *Report of the Committee on Children and Young Persons* (Ingleby Report), Cmnd. 1191, HMSO.
HOME OFFICE (1968) *Report of the Committee on Local Authority and Allied Personal Services* (Seebohm Report), Cmnd. 3703, HMSO.
INGLEBY REPORT *see* HOME OFFICE (1960).
JEFFREYS, M. (1965) *An Anatomy of Social Welfare Services*, Michael Joseph.
JONES, K. (1955) *Law, Lunacy and Conscience 1774-1845*, Routledge & Kegan Paul.
JONES, K. (1966) *The Compassionate Society*, SPCK.
JORDAN, W. K. (1960) *The Charities of London, 1480-1660*, Russell Sage Foundation, Allen & Unwin.
JORNS, A. (1931) *The Quakers as Pioneers in Social Work*, Macmillan.
KAHN, A. J. (1966) *Issues in American Social Work*, Columbia University Press.
KELLEY, A. M. (ed.) (1967) *The Life of Robert Owen Written by Himself*, New York Reprints of Economic Classics.
KENT, J. (1962) *Elizabeth Fry*, Batsford.
KILBRANDON REPORT *see* SCOTTISH HOME AND HEALTH DEPT. (1964).
KIRKMAN-GRAY, B. (1908) *Philanthropy and The State*, King & Sons, London.

KUENSTLER, P. (ed.) (1961) *Community Organisation in Great Britain*, Faber.

LEAPER, R. A. B. (1971) *Community Work*, National Council of Social Service.

LOCH, C. S. (ed.) (1904) *Methods of Social Advance*, Macmillan.

LUBOVE, R. (1966) *The Professional Altruist: The Emergence of Social Work as a Career*, Harvard University Press.

MCKIE, E. (1963) *Venture in Faith*, Liverpool Family Service Unit.

MCLAUGHLIN, B. (ed.) (1969) *Studies in Social Movements: A Social/Psychological Perspective*, Free Press.

MINISTRY OF EDUCATION (1960) *The Youth Service in England and Wales* (Albemarle Report), Cmnd. 929, HMSO.

MINISTRY OF HEALTH (1954) *Circular 27/54*, Cmnd. 9566, HMSO.

MINISTRY OF HEALTH (1959) *Report of the Working Party on Social Workers in the Local Authority Health and Welfare Services* (Younghusband Report), HMSO.

MORGAN, J. S. (ed.) (1966) *Welfare and Wisdom*, University of Toronto Press.

MORRIS, C. (ed.) (1949, reprinted 1955) *Social Casework in Great Britain*, Faber.

MORRIS, M. (1969) *Voluntary Work in the Welfare State*, Routledge & Kegan Paul.

MOWAT, C. L. (1961) *The Charity Organisation Society*, Methuen.

OWEN, D. (1965) *English Philanthropy, 1660-1960*, Oxford University Press.

PACKMAN, J. (1969) *Child Care Needs and Numbers*, Allen & Unwin.

PARKER, J. (1965) *Local Health and Welfare Services*, Allen & Unwin.

PEERS, C. J. (1955) Letter to *The Times*, London, 23 March.

PINKER, R. (1971) *Social Theory and Social Policy*, Heinemann.

POLANYI, K. (1957) *The Great Transformation*, Beacon Press.

REASON, W. (ed.) (1898) *University and Social Settlements*, Methuen.

RICHMOND, M. (1915, reprinted 1965) *Social Diagnosis*, Collier-Macmillan.

ROSE, M. E. (1971) *The English Poor Law 1780-1930*, David & Charles.

ROWNTREE, B. S. and LAVERS, G. N. (1951) *Poverty and the Welfare State*, Longmans.

RUBENSTEIN, D. and SIMON, B. (1968) *The Evolution of the Comprehensive School*, Routledge & Kegan Paul.

SCHOTTLAND, C. I. (ed.) (1967) *The Welfare State*, Harper & Row.

SCOTTISH HOME AND HEALTH DEPT. (1964) *Report of the Committee on Children and Young Persons (Scotland)* (Kilbrandon Report), Cmnd. 2306, HMSO.

SEEBOHM REPORT *see* HOME OFFICE (1968).

SEED, P. (1966) *The Psychological Problem of Disarmament*, Housmans.

'SLEEPTITE FLASH' (Internal Newsletter of Family Service Units), unpublished, 1955 (March/April, May/June, Sept./Oct., Nov./Dec.); 1956 (Nov./Dec.); 1957 (March/April, Sept./Oct.); 1958 (July/Aug.); 1960 (March/April).

SMITH, M. (1965) *Professional Education for Social Work*, Allen & Unwin.

SOCIAL WORK SERVICES GROUP (SCOTLAND) (1968) *Circular S.W.6*.

STEPHENS, T. (1946) *Problem Families*, Pacifist Service Units.

TAWNEY, R. H. (1964) *The Radical Tradition*, Allen & Unwin.

TIMMS, N. (1964) *Psychiatric Social Work in Great Britain (1939-62)*, Routledge & Kegan Paul.

TITMUSS, R. M. (1958) *Essays on the Welfare State*, Allen & Unwin.

TOYNBEE HALL (1891) 7th *Annual Report*; (1898) 14th *Annual Report*; (1899) 15th *Annual Report*.

TOYNBEE RECORD (October 1889) Vol. 2, No. 1; (April 1890) Vol. 2, No. 7, Toynbee Hall.

WATSON, SHERIFF W. (1851) *The Juvenile Vagrant and the Industrial School, or Prevention is Better than Cure*, George Davidson, Aberdeen.

WATSON, SHERIFF W. (1876) *Pauperism in Aberdeenshire*, Blackwood.

WATSON, SHERIFF W. (1880) *Vagrancy in Scotland*, Blackwood.

WEBB, B. (1948) *Our Partnership*, Longmans.

WILENSKY, H. and LEBAUX, C. N. (1965) *Industrial Society and Social Welfare*, Collier-Macmillan.

WILLCOCKS, A. (1967) *The Creation of the National Health Service*, Routledge & Kegan Paul.

WILLIAMS, G. (1967) *Caring for People*, National Council of Social Service, Allen & Unwin.

WITNEY, J. (1937) *Elizabeth Fry, Quaker Heroine*, Harrap.

WOODROOFE, K. (1966) *From Charity to Social Work*, Routledge & Kegan Paul.

WOOTTON, B. (1959) *Social Science and Social Pathology*, Allen & Unwin.

YOUNG, A. and ASHTON, E. T. (1956) *British Social Work in the Nineteenth Century*, Routledge & Kegan Paul.

YOUNG, M. and WILLMOTT, P. (1957) *Family and Kinship in East London*, Routledge & Kegan Paul.

YOUNGHUSBAND, E. L. (1947) *Report on the Employment and Training of Social Workers*, Carnegie U.K. Trust, Constable.

YOUNGHUSBAND, E. L. (ed.) (1968) *Education for Social Work*, Allen & Unwin.

YOUNGHUSBAND REPORT *see* MINISTRY OF HEALTH (1959).